GUIDE TO THE UNDERWATER

GUIDE
to the
UNDERWATER

By Bill Slosky and Art Walker

BONANZA BOOKS • NEW YORK

ACKNOWLEDGMENTS

The authors want to express their sincere gratitude to people in various parts of the world whose efforts have materially aided in the preparation of this book. Without the help of many diving friends and organizations who have lent assistance whenever needed, this volume would not have been possible.

Special thanks go to Jean-Jacques Nathan of Editions Fernand Nathan, Paris; Jean Blitz—Le Club Méditerranée, Paris; "Banane" and the Moniteurs at Cadaques, Spain; The Coral Fishermen of the Costa Brava—Pedro Compas and Eusebio Arderiu, Gerona, Spain; André Tanguy and Dr. Paul Merer, Brest, France; and Gilbert Patriti, Marseilles.

Also to the following people who provided special equipment and services: Mares-Rapallo, Rapallo, Italy; Montres Rolex, Geneva, Switzerland; Bolex-Paillard, St. Croix, Switzerland; Jordan Klein, Underwater, Inc., Miami; Sportsways, Inc., Paramount, California; Nivada Watch Co., Grenchen, Switzerland; Little Switzerland, St. Thomas, Virgin Islands; Fenzy, Paris, France; Gerald H. Nieberg, Photographer (for the photo of one of the authors, on page 169); Nikon Division of Nippon Kogaku K.K., Tokyo, Japan.

A note of appreciation is due the "Underwater Naturalist," bulletin of The American Littoral Society; and to the Institute of Marine Science, University of Miami.

Sincere thanks are in order to all our friends in St. Thomas, Virgin Islands, who were always willing when a photo was needed and gave much of their time and effort. Special thanks go to Henry and Berit Reynolds, Owen and Bruce Weddle, Jack and Denise Kahn, Dr. Malcolm Marshall, Bob Czukoski, Ed and Laura Porter, Al White, José Jimenez, Jack and Diane Dobbs, Lyle "Buddy" Copenhaver, Frank Lyons, Roland and Bénédicte Grillon, and David Divald. Additional thanks go to Claude Caron of C. & M. Caron, Inc., John Hamber of John Hamber's Aqua-Lung Center, and to Henry Nieves of Paperbook Gallery Book Shop, the man who first suggested this book.

This book is dedicated to
Brenda

NOTE

For the sake of clarity and easy recognition, the popular names of specific fishes, corals, sponges, and other marine life are capitalized in this book; for example, *Gray Snapper*, *Red Coral*, *Azure Sponge*, and *Sea Anemone*. In addition, *fish* is used as a plural when referring to members of one species, and *fishes* when referring to more than one species, or fishes in general.

0-517-105640
Copyright © MCMLXVI by Sterling Publishing Co., Inc.
Library of Congress Catalog Card Number: 66-16195
All rights reserved. No part of this book may be reproduced
or utilized in any form or by any means, electronic or mechanical,
including photocopying, recording, or by any information storage
and retrieval system, without permission in writing from the
publisher. Inquiries should be addressed to: Bonanza Books,
a division of Crown Publishers, Inc., 419 Park Avenue South,
New York, New York 10016.
This edition is published by Bonanza Books,
a division of Crown Publishers, Inc.
by arrangement with Sterling Publishing Co., Inc.
abcdefgh
Manufactured in the United States of America.

CONTENTS

Even the non-swimmer can enjoy the beauty and fascination of the underwater world by watching through the glass porthole of a floating raft. A raft can serve as a rest and rally point for snorkelers.

SKIN DIVING

FOR PLEASURE

For man, there has always been the enchantment of exploring the unknown—the exciting prospect of discovering a new world. The oceans and everything in them have held a fascination from as far back as time itself. For most people the sea begins and ends at the shore, but for the skin diver endless boundaries lead from the surface downward and outward—expanding to depths of adventure and discovery.

For the enthusiastic skin diver, or anyone interested in the sea, these past few years have revealed many new discoveries because never before has so much energy and interest been devoted to the exploration of the sea and its resources. This new awareness of the sea means we must learn the few simple rules and guiding techniques of underwater swimming.

With modern diving equipment readily available, an underwater swimmer may now feel secure and comfortable in an element that was once reserved entirely for fish and other marine creatures. He can now leisurely explore the silent beauty of

Fish have a great sense of curiosity, and if you approach them slowly, avoiding sudden movements, you can observe them closely. Here a Queen Angelfish comes face-to-face with the hard-shelled Shellfish.

the underwater scene in the shallows of almost any body of water—for lakes, rivers and quarries as well as the sea provide the snorkeler with boundless areas for exploration.

Until recent years, sport divers were looked upon as somewhat eccentric, with a public image that left much to be desired. Now, however, skin diving has become the world's fastest growing sport. No longer is the thrill and exhilaration of "flying" through a weightless world reserved for a select few. The new legion of skin divers has discovered the underwater world as a place of breathtaking beauty, inhabited not by terrible sea monsters and frightful dangers, but by friendly creatures, and with dangers no greater than in the daily existence of our modern "civilized" world.

To explore the submarine world you don't have to be an ex-Channel swimmer or professional diver, or anything close to this. Being able to swim is helpful, but even non-swimmers

Capturing small fishes and other marine specimens is easily accomplished with a slurp-gun. Its sucking action draws in water, and along with it the fish you want to collect.

can learn to explore by using snorkel-boards and other floating units with built-in windows for viewing. Snorkeling covers a great range of capabilities and interests, appealing to both men and women, and even whole families—bringing high adventure to all.

From the mountains, deserts, plains, and sea coasts, skin divers are on the move, travelling thousands of miles in search of "holidays beneath the sea." With the tremendous popularity of diving, water-resort areas around the world are offering interesting facilities to the underwater enthusiast who prefers to venture abroad in search of sun, different diving conditions, scenery, clearer waters, and all the other fascinations of a diving adventure.

Perhaps the best known of the diving resorts is the Club Méditerranée, a French organization offering holiday villages in such romantic spots as Greece, Morocco, Israel, Yugoslavia,

Corsica, Spain, Sicily, Italy, and even Tahiti! The Club's village at Palinuro, Italy, just south of Naples, has the largest diving school in Europe and is second-to-none in the training of novice divers.

Underwater swimming may include fishing, exploration and recognition of marine life, treasure hunting, or even travel adventure. It is up to you. But whatever your interest, you are certain to find the underwater world fascinating, mysterious, full of excitement and adventure—a colorful ever-changing world, so enchanting that you will never cease to wonder how you have stayed away from it so long.

Prepare yourself for a trip with us; a journey through a realm of indescribable beauty, a world you may never have dreamed existed, where your eyes will see forms and dazzling colors and rhythms in movement found nowhere else, a region where venture becomes infinite adventure—where man can make the whole marine world his.

To take a specimen the size of this Red Hind, a member of the Grouper family, use your speargun, or—better still—your camera.

Sportsmanship is the rule underwater! Never spear a lobster. Instead, learn to use a snare, and you will add much to your enjoyment.

Your basic equipment will be mask, snorkel, and swim fins. If you care to bring something back for lunch, take along a speargun or lobster snare. Or maybe you would prefer to gather some specimens for your shell collection or aquarium. In that case, bring a net or slurp-gun. You might wish to take some pictures. The corals and fishes are magnificent, and, who knows, you might even discover a shipwreck! Ancient relics, long hidden by the sea, and important artifacts that complete historical collections, fill museums and add to our knowledge of history, have been discovered by skin divers wearing the simplest basic equipment.

In the Mediterranean, ancient Roman and Greek amphoræ are constantly being recovered as more and more people add diving to their recreational interests.

In this watery domain, animals resemble plants and plants take on an appearance of stone. Decorative fishes are arrayed in startling designs. Here swim the angels, butterflies, wrasses, surgeons—as well as trumpetfish with long spatular beaks and speckled transparent arched tails. The barracuda is an elongated pike with something of the reptile about it. The rocky mass is all life and movement. There are hosts of immature oceanic shapes—flecks of color in every shade of the spectrum. Drift with us through the underwater world!

Before you dive, check the time, think about it, then forget it. Time loses all meaning in this world below the surface. You will find yourself spending literally hours picking your way through this wonderland of bizarre forms and colors, with

At the start, a snorkeler is so engrossed in the panorama of underwater life, that he fails to notice all of its intricate parts. But as time goes on, his senses develop and he becomes increasingly aware of the many distinct forms and patterns of life that compose the world under the sea.

Although the snorkeler may not set out looking for treasure, he may discover it by chance. Here, around this sunken ship, marine life abounds.

stops here and there to collect or to photograph a particularly interesting scene or specimen. Is it any wonder that underwater exploration has been described as the most exciting sport of all?

DIVING TECHNIQUES

Although modern diving equipment is truly fantastic in its function, no equipment produced can overcome the feeling of insecurity which some swimmers feel in the water. An air-tank (variously called "aqualung" and "scuba," for self-contained underwater breathing apparatus) often compensates for an individual's deficiency in swimming skills. But in an emergency, perhaps resulting in the accidental loss of the air-tank or necessitating intentional abandoning of it in order to surface more quickly, the heavily equipped diver has to revert to being a swimmer with nothing but his innate ability to carry him back to safety. Your mask, fins, and snorkel will give greater comfort and flexibility in the water, but the extent to which they help you is dependent on your aptitude in swimming. A good water technique, not style so much as ease and confidence, plus a fair physical condition are as essential as the equipment itself. Equipment will not make you a good diver but, with experience and a little concentrated effort, mask, fins, and snorkel will readily assist you in discovering this new and exciting underwater frontier.

A snorkeler discovers the enchantment of gliding smoothly through a sponge-encrusted archway.

There are two important effects of underwater pressure that you, the snorkel diver, must keep in mind. The first, inner ear squeeze, is experienced as a "wedged-in" sensation while descending. This feeling is a good indication that the pressure in the inner ear is not being equalized properly. The air pressure in the inner ear must be "equal" to the surrounding water pressure at whatever depth you are. If not balanced within 6 to 8 feet of the surface, pain and possible ear damage could result, as the air in the middle ear is trapped at surface pressure. The purpose of clearing (equalizing) is to open the Eustachian tubes and let pressurized air in the lungs flow to the middle ear, thus keeping the eardrum in a state of equilibrium.

Equalize or "pop" your ears by swallowing, or holding your nostrils closed and blowing your nose, or by using both techniques simultaneously. You will learn proper equalizing techniques only with practice and patience—and later, in the Spearfishing Phase, you will discover a method of rapid equalization employed by many underwater hunters along the Mediterranean coast.

While finning along the surface with your mask and snorkel in place, you can view the scenery below or scan the bottom for fishes or treasure.

The second phenomenon of squeeze you may experience is mask squeeze. This condition is like that of a vacuum and occurs when the air pressure within the face mask is less than that of the external water pressure.

The depth at which mask squeeze occurs depends upon how much air is in the mask at the beginning of the dive. As you descend, the air pressure in the mask lowers, allowing the water pressure to force the mask lens up against your nose. To correct it, simply exhale into your mask until the air pressure inside equals the air pressure outside. Then instantly push the mask back to its normal position.

Wearing a face-mask is a must, for without it your eyes will see everything out of focus. Remember that the mask makes objects appear one-third larger and distances one-fourth nearer. Your diving mask is your magic window to the sea, so take special care in selecting one that fits properly and has features that aid, not restrict, your diving. Steer clear of combination mask-snorkels, unless you intend to limit your observation to a swimming pool—and even then they are not particularly recommended. A float or valve mechanism is attached to the snorkel tube of combination mask-snorkels. This is designed to close over the opening of the tube, sealing water out. Too often, however, these types leak when in certain positions. The danger is in the natural tendency to gasp a large breath of air when emerging from a dive. If the position of the diver is such that the snorkel-tube valves are not fully open, or remain closed, there is the possibility that the seals will be sucked shut by the diver. When you surface from a dive, you want air, not problems!

Look for a mask made of fairly soft rubber, with a sturdy headstrap, a metal binding rim, and feather-edge or neoprene seal. Test your mask for proper sealing by placing it on your face without the headstrap. The bottom of the mask should fit under your nose. Inhale gently through the nose. This should cause a partial vacuum inside the mask, and if it fits well without your holding it, it means no air has been able to enter; therefore, no water will seep through when later submerged, and the seal is good. Don't wait until you are at the beach to make this test—do it when purchasing the mask. Be sure to choose a mask with clear shatterproof glass; plastic lenses tend to fog and become easily scratched. If you should need corrective lenses, these, too, are available and can be fitted into most masks.

We are all familiar with the fogging of a car's windows when exposed to cool temperatures. The same problem is caused by breath when breathing into a face-mask that has been suddenly exposed to the cool temperatures of the water. The condensation on the inside lens can be prevented very easily. Though there are a few commercially available aids that can be used for the purpose of de-fogging, the easiest and most readily available product is saliva. Its protein content has the same effect. Simply "spit" on the inside of the face-plate, rub over the entire surface of the glass, and then lightly rinse in water. Your fogging problems will be solved!

As equalizing of inner ear pressure will have to be accomplished with your mask in place (and swallowing does not work for everyone), make certain the mask you purchase has either a nose-pinching device incorporated into it, or a soft rubber pad which can be pushed up against the nostrils, closing them off. With either of these two systems, exhaling through the nose facilitates rapid clearing of the ears.

The only other "extra" now available in most diving-masks is a purge valve. Should water accidentally enter the mask, a slight exhalation through the nose will easily purge water from the mask. This valve operates on a one-way system: a rubber flap permits air to escape, but prevents any water from entering. This is often referred to as a non-return valve. Both a nose-pinching device and a purge valve are valuable assets to your diving-mask.

Those who have experienced the exhausting cycle of trying

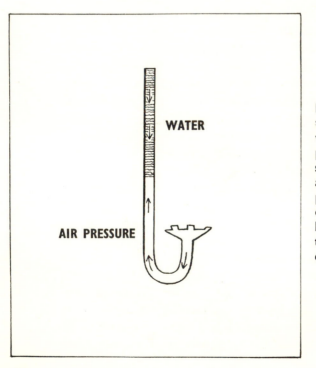

WATER

AIR PRESSURE

By holding your breath when submerging, water will come only part way down the snorkel tube. The air already in the tube prevents its flooding completely, so one hard blow after returning to the surface should clear the snorkel.

to swim underwater without the aid of a snorkel know well the discomfort of constantly having to turn to gulp a breath of air, having your feet sink, and then having to give an added kick simply to maintain buoyancy. The open end "J" tube is the best and simplest snorkel to use (*see page* 18). This type permits you to float along the surface with your face down, slightly submerged, and breathing easily through the tube. The only effort required to maintain this position for literally hours is slight expansion of the chest and diaphragm muscles to overcome a light pressure that is not even noticeable to the snorkeler.

One end of the snorkel is above the water, the other, fitted with a comfortable mouthpiece of rubber or plastic, is gripped firmly in your mouth. Your lips form a watertight seal around the flange of the mouthpiece. Don't bite hard on it, only just enough to prevent the snorkel from slipping out of your mouth.

As a snorkel diver, when you spot something on the bottom worth investigating, draw in a deep breath and dive. During the dive, of course, you must hold your breath. This means that when you surface, the snorkel will be filled with water that must be removed before you resume normal breathing. Clear the tube by "spitting" the used air from your lungs through the snorkel. The sudden blast of air will completely clear the tube of water and permit you to inhale a water-free breath. Use this same "clearing" technique for any water that splashes into the snorkel while you are observing from the surface. An all-rubber snorkel is recommended. If you prefer not to attach the tube to the strap of your face-mask, then put it under the strap, which will hold it well in place.

Swim fins will greatly increase your forward motion, manoeuvrability, and swimming efficiency. Design of the fins should be such that it affords a comfortable fit. Take the same care in your choice of fins that you would in buying a pair of dress shoes. Keep in mind that the primary purpose of fins is to give medium speed in the water with a minimum of effort. Color is really a matter of individual taste.

Whether or not you should buy floating fins usually depends on the normal visibility of waters in your diving area. If the waters are quite clear and calm, a non-floating fin can easily be seen should it drop to the bottom. However, if you enter the

1. Your most efficient source of propulsion is the flutter kick. Keep knees slightly bent and arms at sides. Advance with a pedalling movement of the feet.

2. Execute the duck-dive by first taking a deep breath. Then bend at the waist and thrust yourself downward with a pulling motion of the arms.

3. Lift your legs straight up into the air and let the weight of your legs push you below the surface. By wearing sufficient weights, you can conserve energy during the dive.

4 and 5.
Do not begin to kick until your fins are entirely submerged. After gaining an initial momentum, relax and drift lazily downward, resembling the motion of a falling leaf. Continue your descent using a flutter kick.

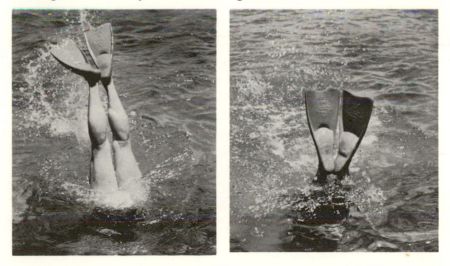

6. As you descend, bring your free hand sharply to your side for momentum. "Equalize" ear pressure by pressing mask firmly against nose, or pinch the nose-pinching device and exhale gently.

water from a rough beach or where an object on the bottom is not easily seen from the surface, the floating type of fin is best.

Let your particular physical condition determine if you should choose fins with flexible blades or fins with rigid blades. If you have strong leg muscles and a lot of stamina, large rigid-bladed fins are best for you, but be honest with yourself—you are the one who has to wear them.

Some type of flotation equipment is necessary for all skin divers. Important as a "rest and rally point," it is useful in reaching a diving spot far from shore, or to carry game, specimens collected, and additional equipment. Good flotation devices currently in use are inner-tubes of good rubber, surfmats, paddleboards, and even small boats.

7. Forget about your arms—stroking with your arms causes drag and requires much more energy than the added speed it provides. Continue leisurely in order not to consume an excess of oxygen nor miss the extravagant beauty of the submarine garden.

8. After coming up from a dive, exhale sharply to clear water from the snorkel. With practice you will be able to do this as the snorkel tube "breaks" water, and be ready to dive again within a breath or two.

Your knife is a very important tool. Look for one with a 5- to 7-inch blade of good stainless steel. Make sure its construction is heavy enough to withstand prying and pounding, and that the blade is sharp enough to cut through most entanglements (i.e., nets, lines, kelp, and even large speared fish that could hamper your ascent to the surface). Remember that the diving knife is not considered an offensive weapon and should not be purchased for such use.

To offset the body's natural buoyancy, most divers wear a set of weights around the waist. As the buoyancy of each individual varies, the right amount of weight can only be determined by trial and error. Carry only enough extra poundage to allow a slight positive buoyancy: when underwater you will rise slowly; when exhaling you will sink slowly. These extra few pounds will allow you to dive and still conserve energy that would normally be spent. Make certain you wear a belt that features a safety or "quick-release" buckle. Should you have to jettison your weight-belt in an emergency, give a simple pull on the buckle and the entire belt will fall away.

The last piece of supplementary equipment is probably the one least considered by most snorkel divers, but a pair of cotton work gloves protects your hands from sharp rocks, coral, and any fish or marine specimens you bring back from your snorkeling promenade. If you decide on a leather-palmed pair rather than cotton, be sure they allow you the necessary "touch" required for pinching off the nose in clearing the ears, and dexterity in handling other pieces of equipment such as a speargun, slurp-gun, or camera.

With your equipment in correct position and an experienced diver alongside, you are now ready to begin the first of many exciting and eventful swims on and below the transparent door to adventure.

You must stay on the surface initially, until you are accustomed to breathing through the snorkel. *DON'T* breathe naturally. Deep breathing gives greater buoyancy, keeps the body higher on the surface, and lessens the chance of water entering the snorkel. Your particular breathing rate will develop with experience. Practice dipping the snorkel underwater, then clearing it by blowing hard, never lifting your head above the surface.

Keep your arms next to your body as you move along the surface. Swim with a slow, steady flutter kick, keeping the knees as straight as possible. Fins should be just below the surface, to prevent splashing as you move slowly along.

Practice flooding your mask while you are on the surface, and clearing it by holding the uppermost part of the mask firmly against your face and exhaling through the nose.

Learn your basic, practical diving with mask, snorkel, and fins before venturing with "scuba" (self-contained underwater breathing apparatus). The underwater world is a beautiful and inviting place, but it can quickly become a very hostile environment to the diver who is not properly trained in the use of underwater breathing equipment. Seek instruction from a qualified instructor.

SPEARFISHING

Once you have become addicted to the pastime of snorkeling, it is very probable you will want to try another phase of free-diving that is somewhat more demanding than fish-watching; this is spearfishing. Here is a combination individual- and team-sport that offers a degree of challenge not found in any other. It requires skill, endurance, and an acute awareness of personal limitations.

The skill involved includes the development of an "eye" sufficiently keen to observe a fish like the grouper camouflaged on a bottom 40 feet below; a knowledge of the habits of different species of fish and likely spots to find them; and finally, the ability, when within range, to sight accurately and squeeze off a "stoning" brain or spinal shot.

As preparation for a snorkel dive, most spearfishermen "hyperventilate," or force-breathe, as standard procedure. Hyperventilation helps you stay underwater much longer and is even said to double your time if done properly. It consists of a series of forced breaths, during which the lungs are *completely*

Stalking methods vary according to the type of fish you are hunting. With experience, the appropriate technique will come naturally. To bag a Red Snapper the waiting method often works best. Since snappers are extremely curious, you can go quite close to them, but you must remain very still if they approach. Frequently these fishes will swim up to within a few inches of your spear.

emptied and filled. This purges the blood stream of carbon dioxide, as well as the lungs, and saturates the blood with oxygen. By hyperventilating in this manner for several minutes before a dive, you can hold your breath for extended periods. Keep in mind, however, that *excessive* hyperventilation can be extremely dangerous, as you are consciously repressing the urge to return to the surface for a new breath of air, and there is always the possibility of being overcome by anoxia (oxygen starvation), more commonly known as "blacking-out." In moderation, however, hyperventilation is a great aid to snorkel divers.

In 1960, a Sicilian skin diver named Enzo Maiorca set a snorkel-diving record of 160.7 feet in the clear waters off Ognina, near Syracuse, Sicily. Except for his mask, fins and

Always try for a "stone" or kill shot. The spear should strike the fish's brain or spinal column. Your target should be the area behind and slightly above the eye. You will find that a certain satisfaction accompanies a direct "stone shot."

snorkel, Maiorca was aided only by a speargun ballasted with 11 pounds of lead. Almost unbelievable, but true!

Many of the European divers are now employing his weighting method as a means of conserving energy and increasing efficiency, particularly when descending to great depths with simple snorkel equipment. But there is no reason why this same technique cannot be practiced in shallow waters, with the diver enjoying longer bottom-time. Ballast your speargun with strips of lead weight; tie one end of a long thin line to the handle of the gun and the other end to the float that you are working from (here a sturdy rubber inner tube is great). While you scan the bottom for game, rest the gun on the float. When you locate the fish, glide easily downward with weighted gun in hand, take your shot and drop the gun or fish. Return to the surface, get your breath, pull up the gun, and with good luck (or skill) the fish as well! This process can be repeated over and over during a day's dive. Remember,

As a spearfisherman, you'll seek this Nassau Grouper in caves, under ledges, and even camouflaged on the open bottom. Though this 20-pounder has many color phases, the dark spot (caudal) at the base of the tail does not change, which makes the species readily identifiable.

however, this is only one of many techniques spearfishermen employ. Learn them all, and then use the one that's best for you in your particular area.

Spearfishing, like flying a plane, takes place in an element basically unnatural to man. Aircraft have certain limitations as to range, manoeuvrability, and speed and a pilot must be aware of these at all times. In the same way, every diver has certain limits of which we should always be aware. The penalty for exceeding these bounds can be severe. While hunting underwater, situations arise in which you are tempted to step beyond a safe range. *Don't take the risk.*

Your equipment for spearfishing is basic snorkel gear plus a gun, and you will probably find a rubber "wet-jacket" good protection from fish spines, coral, and, over an extended period, cold water. If you are not diving in tropical or semi-tropical waters, then a "wet-suit" is necessary regardless of duration in the water.

Once you have spotted your fish, glide in quietly for the final approach. Sight fine and, at exactly the right moment, squeeze the trigger. Remember when timing your shot that everything in the water is magnified and distances are actually greater than they appear.

As for spearguns, there are several different styles, but they can all be classified according to their source of power: spring; CO_2 and pneumatic, which are both air-powered; and rubber. The rubber-powered guns include the arbalete, Hawaiian-sling, and sea-lance. Selecting a gun, is, to an extent, a matter of individual taste; however, simplicity of construction and cost of maintenance are important. The fishing area and the kind of fish you intend to take should also be considered. (It might be noted that CO_2 guns are not allowed in tournament competition.)

Spearheads for any of the previously mentioned guns are interchangeable, and for those not intended for use on competitors' spearguns, adaptors are available. A spearhead with angular sides has much more penetrating power than a round pointed tip and is much easier to sharpen. For big fishes with tremendous twisting power like jacks, barracuda, tarpon and sharks, use a "fall-away" or detachable head. This spearhead is connected to the harpoon (spear) by a wire cable. Once the

If your shot turns out not to be a kill, get to the fish as quickly as possible. If you think it is going to tear loose from the spear, grab the fish—don't risk losing your prize to the scavengers of the sea. Wear a pair of gloves as protection against spines. (The white spots in the picture are reflections of the flash off plankton through the camera lens.)

Remove a speared fish from the water as soon as possible. In tropical waters particularly there is a chance of the blood or vibration of the fish attracting a shark or barracuda. Note that the spear went through the fish's gill to its brain, killing it instantly.

point is embedded in the fish, the head slips off the spear preventing him from bending that valuable shaft into a figure-eight! The head and the cable will hold the fish until you can force him to the surface, boat him, or tuck him safely into the bag on your float.

A last note regarding equipment for spearfishing: If you are not hunting in deep water where the bottom is something less than the familiar obstacle course of the coral reef, then you are probably carrying too much line on your speargun. You will rarely hit a fish beyond one and a half spear lengths away, so make this adjustment to the length of line between your spear shaft and gun. Two full lengths of the spear is an adequate length, and you won't waste time with tangled lines.

Remember that a speargun has a safety-catch, so use it. A

When going in for a strike, have the gun in spearing position because last minute preparations will often "spook" (frighten away) the fish. Take special care when shooting a barracuda because the fish is potentially dangerous. Here a spearfisherman has positioned a cuda for a "stone shot."

gun for underwater hunting should be handled with the same caution as any weapon. In spearfishing, load the gun *after* entering the water, and unload it *before* leaving the water. This applies to beach diving as well as swimming from a boat.

At this point, you should know that in many countries spearfishing with the aid of underwater breathing equipment (scuba) is forbidden. Even in areas where there is a feeling of indifference towards spearfishing, it is an unwritten law among the divers that the hunter must return to the surface for air, remaining essentially in his own element while the fishes remain in theirs. Here, then, the spearfisherman must rely upon his skill in diving and his knowledge of the activity pattern of fish.

Find outlying areas for your hunting, remembering that even a small amount of spearing tends to make fishes grow wary or drives them off to deep waters. This will leave easily accessible waters for non-spearfishermen, naturalists, and photographers. And, of course, never spear small, non-game fishes such as Angelfishes, Butterfly Fishes, and other lovely coral dwellers.

To make your first spearfishing trip a success, a few basic pointers are in order. To begin, move smoothly and silently through the water, with the tip of your speargun pointing downward, and its safety-catch on. Avoid any sudden movements, as fish are curious by nature. If you use a slow pursuit, you can approach most fishes.

Some experienced spearfishermen swim on their side at the surface, thus eliminating bubbles from their swim fins that

A spearfisherman can be proud of boating the very game and fast-moving "Great" Barracuda. A live shark or barracuda is a potential danger in a boat. Stay away from its snapping jaws until it is definitely dead.

One of the skills of spearfishing is knowing likely spots to find fish. This wreck serves as a refuge for fishes of all descriptions. Look into darkened holes for the big ones. Stalk your prey quietly.

would normally be visible below. Each spearfisherman that you meet will probably have some tips that have helped him as an underwater hunter. Again, try to learn them all.

For a silent entry, try the feet-first vertical dive. Starting from the water surface, raise your body with a driving kick and downward stroke of your hands. As you drop back below the surface, jackknife and complete your dive. Some divers remove their snorkel when making such a dive, as this will perhaps prevent bubbles from frightening the fish.

There are certain techniques for different species of fish, such as the rock fish—Groupers, Margates, Breams, which live in caves and beneath rocks. These are fish that generally "home" in a certain area. Then there are the pelagic or open-water fishes such as Jacks, Snappers, Mackerel, and Tarpon. Also frequently speared are the bottom-fish like Flounders, Sole, and Rays. These are usually found on the flat bottom, often buried in the sand and are difficult to spot from the surface.

When you sight a Nassau Grouper, dive straight down on him (if weighted with an extra pound or two, you will be able to fall right on to the fish). The Nassau will be momentarily hypnotized by your downward approach; glide in quietly, sight fine, and squeeze off the shot. In timing your shot, remember that everything before you is magnified and the distance is actually greater than it appears. When, then, is the right moment? When you feel you are approximately a spear length away, shoot.

For the Nassau you will be diving straight towards his head. Estimate the distance between his eyes; then calculate an equal distance vertically so that you have formed a triangle. That will give you a shot behind and slightly above the eye, in other words, a "brain-shot." If executed properly, you will only have to pull the fish to the surface. If your shot is not a kill, however, get to the fish as quickly as possible. If you think he is about to tear loose from the spear, grab him by the eye-sockets (this is when you will be thankful for gloves) and swim to the surface. In tropical waters, low-frequency vibrations from a struggling fish will quickly attract any Shark or Barracuda in the area, so get all fishes out of the water immediately after shooting.

This fisherman is about to boat his speared catch. The ideal way to hold a speared fish is by gripping the eyes firmly. Do not depend upon the spear to hold the fish.

When spearfishing from a boat, hand your fish with the spear in it to the boatman. Don't try to remove the spear in the water.

For the Black Grouper, Margate, or Mediterranean Bream which usually like to "hole-up," a different approach is needed. Once you have spotted your fish, try to coax him into a darkened area—a shadow or even a small hole. These fish evidently feel secure in a dark environment and are more approachable there.

With the Bream, who usually lives in the shallows beneath rocks in mid-summer, you must dive, aim, and fire very quickly, or he will soon be too far back into his hole to reach. If this happens, though, you might try making scratching noises with the tip of your speargun on a rock. Most rock fish will usually come out to investigate, and then you must be quick!

Another good technique used to entice a big fish from his cavernous lodging is to crush mussels or sea urchins outside the entrance. (Attracting fish by the use of such bait is known as "chumming.") Then hang vertically (with your feet above your head) above the opening and wait for the fish to come out to investigate. Does this sound too difficult? Actually, it is easier than making horizontal shots, as you are less buoyant and have better control when your fins are above you.

There is a classic underwater hunter's trick for the fish which has been shot and has lodged in a hole. Brace your feet up against the rock or coral head and heave the fish out from its rocky retreat. Do this by taking hold of the fish by the eyes, your fingers getting a solid grip in the deep eye cavities. This is enough to paralyze the fish to some extent, even a big one, so that you can yank it out without the time- and energy-consuming "playing" of the fish.

For the free-swimming fishes there is still another excellent technique. Here, again, this deals with chumming. Shoot a small fish, tie it to your float and let it rest on the border between the upper and lower depths, just to attract others. The other fishes tend to lose their usual mistrust of spearguns, and will often circle round and round the corpse. Dive down to the bottom, stretch out your arms and stay motionless until a fish comes into your line of fire. Again, if you are in tropical or semi-tropical waters, using fish for chumming is the quickest way to bring sharks or barracuda to the area, so be extra cautious and alert. Keep your diving companion within sight at all times.

Standing casually in 80 feet of water and leisurely loading his speargun, this spearfisherman is guilty of breaking the sport's code of ethics by using an aqualung. Scuba is not permitted in spearfishing contests, and in some areas scuba gear as an aid to spearfishing is forbidden by law.

Above, two proud
spearfishermen display
their catch by properly
holding the fishes by
the eyesockets.

During a tournament,
points are scored
according to size and
type of fish. This
Hogfish weighed in at
13 pounds.

Local laws forbid spearfishing in most lakes, although carp, gar and suckers are normally open game. However, there certainly are no prohibitions against studying and photographing interesting feeding and activity patterns or habits of the other fresh-water fishes.

After spearfishing became popular in the late 1940's, interest in the sport brought about the founding of the International Spearfishing Association, to set up rules governing international contests. Besides the Annual International Spearfishing Championships, many local tournaments are held in various parts of the world each year.

One of the most exciting parts of any spearfishing tournament is the "weigh-in." Points are tallied on the basis of size and type of catch, as well as difficulty in spearing.

As a spearfisherman, use sound judgment in selecting the kind and quality of game to be taken. Be concerned with conservation—one who enjoys the beauty of nature should be interested in preserving it. Shoot only what you intend to use. Good hunting!

Spearing a "Permit" Jack is a double thrill. It will not only add many points to your tournament score, but this fish makes a tasty dish on the dinner table. Jacks are usually rated high in point value because they are fast and wily.

The Moon Jellyfish with its clover-leaf emblem drifts over the mask of the diver.

A tiny Bluehead Wrasse swims gaily past a large Brain Coral.

MARINE LIFE – FISHES

Popular names of fishes are often confusing, to say the least. For this reason, we have included scientific names wherever possible. Stressing correct family relationships, also, should tend to reduce misunderstandings about the common names of many fishes.

Probably the most decorative of marine creatures you will observe during your snorkeling excursions are the reef dwellers. You will be dazzled by the conspicuous and vivid colors and bizarre forms of the bodies and appendages of these marine animals. Colors of the fishes are understandable if you consider changes in their activities. The schools sport the bright hues of the tropical reef; these markings may serve as identifying insignia so that each species may school with its own kind, or as camouflage against the background colors of corals, sponges, sea fans, and algae. At mating time the reef fishes may don bright pigmented tones, varying the colors from hour to hour.

THE PARROTFISHES—FAMILY *SCARIDAE*

Brilliant colors are characteristic of the Parrotfishes. Gaudily colored with blue, red, green and yellow, the Parrotfishes well earn their name. The teeth are fused into a solid bony plate which somewhat resembles the beak of the parrot. They spend their days about the reef grazing on algae and you may hear them crunching on the coral to reach the algae that grows just beneath the surface of the coral. When the Parrotfish removes food from the coral, it also bites off chunks of the reef, so that it is quite obvious where fishes of this kind have been foraging.

One of the largest of the reef-dwelling fishes, the Parrotfish is also one of the most timid, and close approach is almost impossible. Chopping up a Sea Urchin will sometimes bring them close, but not for long. Darting up to the Urchin, scattering the other reef-fish, the Parrotfish will snatch a piece of Urchin and, with a shake of its head, be gone. It is often seen in the company of Blue Tangs and Doctorfish, and the slightest aggressive movement on your part will send them all scurrying helter-skelter through coral crevices and passages, through tortuous paths, away and out of sight.

There are over eighty species of Parrotfishes the world over;

The Ribbon Parrotfish is a spectacular member of the undersea world.

they are found in the West Indies, on both sides of the Atlantic and in the tropical western Pacific. Some species go through three entirely different color phases making correct identification extremely difficult.

Active during the day, the Parrotfish is one of the few fishes that actually rest or sleep during the night. Certain species, in fact, are known to secrete a gelatinous cocoon of mucus around their body and spend the night tightly wedged under coral ledges. So far, this remarkable biological phenomenon has only been discovered among the Parrotfishes. How and why this cocoon is formed remains a mystery.

Brilliantly marked with orange and green stripes, the Ribbon Parrotfish (*Scarus taeniopterus*) is one of the species known to secrete the mucous envelope around its body at night. The Red Parrotfish (*Sparisoma abildgaardi*), one of the smaller members of this family, grows to less than a foot. Its red and brown body spotted in white makes identification quite easy even to the amateur fish-watcher. Most Parrotfishes are named after their individual color schemes such as the Purple Parrotfish (*Pseudoscarus plumbaeus*), the dark purplish-blue covering the entire body making this species easy to spot. Others, like the

Here two Red Parrotfish are busy feeding on coral.

The sharp teeth of the Parrotfishes allow them to crunch the coral into digestible tidbits.

Rainbow (*Pseudoscarus guacamaia*), Mud (*Sparisoma flavescens*), Stoplight (*Sparisoma viride*), and Queen (*Scarus vetula*), may be more difficult to recognize.

One of the smallest of the Parrotfishes is the Mudbelly, seen here swimming just below a Butterfly Fish.

THE WRASSES—FAMILY *LABRIDAE*

There are over 500 species of Wrasses in the world, ranging from the tiny West Indian Dwarf Wrasse of less than 3 inches (*Lachnolaimus maximus*) to the Tautog (*Tautoga onitis*), common off the U.S. coast from Cape Cod to Delaware; the California Sheepshead (*Pimelometopon pulcher*) which grows to 3 feet and reaches a weight of 25 pounds; and the Cuckoo Wrasse of the Mediterranean (*Labrus ossifagus*). The Wrasses found about the tropical reefs are brightly colored, aggressive little fishes with thick lips and prominent canine-like teeth projecting from their mouths.

This is typical of the swarming habits of the Wrasses.

They often act as "cleaner fishes," removing parasites from the heads and gills of larger fishes who would normally prey on them. The Wrasses remain in a small area and set up cleaning stations where they are visited by their "patients." Groupers, Squirrel Fish, Jacks and even the vicious Moray Eel are among the many fishes that use the services of the cleaner Wrasses. Marine biologists theorize that the Wrasses' job of removing parasites from other fish contributes substantially to the health of marine populations.

On the other hand, the Hawaiian Saddle Wrasse (*Thalassoma*

A Yellowhead Wrasse passes in front of a Red Sponge. On the upper right is Flower Coral.

duperreyi) is known to be a vicious little fish using its incisor-like teeth to attack and mutilate other species and, in some instances, members of its own species.

The Atlantic Bluehead Wrasse (*Thalassoma bifasciatum*) undergoes many marked color changes during its growth. The young Bluehead may be a bright yellow with a dark lateral line, or it may be plain yellow. With growth, the female Bluehead's coloring changes to form broad vertical brown patches. The male, on the other hand, undergoes quite different color changes. Its head becomes a brilliant blue and its body a vibrant green, marked by two thick black bands.

A similar species common in California waters is the Senorita (*Oxyulis californica*). Inhabiting rocks and kelp beds, it is kelp-brown in color with cream below and a black blotch at the base of the tail. This particular species of Wrasse has the unusual habit of sleeping completely submerged in sand.

The Hogfish (*Lachnolaimus maximus*), an excellent food fish, is also a member of the Wrasse family, although it is often mistaken for a snapper (*see page* 38).

The "Slippery Dick" and Razor-fish are perhaps the most abundant of the smaller Wrasses found swarming around the reef and coral heads.

THE GOATFISHES—FAMILY *MULLIDAE*

The Spotted Goatfish (*Upeneus maculatus*) is a tropical fish easily recognized by the two long tactile barbels under its chin. A typical sandy-bottom fish, the Goatfish uses its sensory barbels to explore the bottom and locate food particles. Capable of rapid color changes, the Goatfish has been known to change from mottled red to almost completely white in a few seconds. The Northern Goatfish (*Mullus auratus*) and the Yellow Goatfish (*Upeneus martinicus*) are two related West Indian species. The Red Surmullet of the Mediterranean is also a related species. The only species of Goatfish common to the American West Coast is the *Upeneus dentatus*.

The Spotted Goatfish is a regular inhabitant of the shallow offshore reef areas. You can see these fishes in small schools picking their way across sandy patches between the coral heads. Seemingly absorbed in their hunt for food, they are quite easy to approach, and even when they spot a diver they make no effort to retreat. The Spotted Goatfish in the photo below ignored the approach of the photographer and posed quite willingly for the picture.

A Goatfish searches along the bottom for a meal.

This pair of French Angelfish, seen here at a depth of 80 feet, is cautious and wary of intruders.

THE ANGELFISHES—FAMILY *CHAETODONTIDAE*

Perhaps the most photographed fishes in the sea, the Angelfishes certainly deserve their reputation as the loveliest of all marine creatures.

A particularly handsome West Indian species, the French Angelfish (*Pomacanthus paru*) can be found swimming in small groups in the deeper, darker waters off the reef. Distrusting all skin divers, they turn aloofly away and are gone with a flash of their gilded bodies into the deep. The young French Angelfish have several yellowish bands across their bodies, but these fade as they mature.

The gentle looking Black Angelfish (*Pomacanthus arcuatus*) is a curious and friendly creature. One of the largest Angelfishes, it often reaches two feet in length and travels in groups of two or three. Easily approached, the Black Angelfish will turn and face the diver, swim towards him and veer off when it gets quite close. It sometimes repeats this performance many times. The young Black Angel has distinctive white vertical bars which stripe its body. These fade away as the fish matures,

48

The young Black Angelfish loses its vertical stripes as it matures.

The adult Black Angelfish, most commonly seen by underwater swimmers, presents a pouting face to the camera.

A whole school of Black Angelfish, such as this, is rarely seen.

leaving only the white ring around its mouth, which seems to be pouting constantly.

Truly queens of the underwater world, the regal Queen Angelfish (*Angelichthys ciliaris*) add magnificent color to the

The Rock Beauty is a brilliant blue-eyed member of the Angelfish family.

Queen Angelfish hide in an undersea cave.

underwater scene. Their large predominantly bright yellow bodies are edged with an equally brilliant blue, and they have a dark spot ringed in blue above the eye. This distinguishes them from the Common Angelfish (*Angelichthys isabelita*) which is very similar but does not have this spot. The Queen Angelfish feeds mostly on invertebrates and vegetation, and you will usually find them alone around reefs and rocky places. When you encounter one on your underwater promenade, don't be surprised if it puts on a show for you—twisting and turning to be sure you catch all the splendor of its colors.

Another striking member of the Angelfish family is the Rock Beauty (*Holacanthus tricolor*). You will recognize this Caribbean and southern Atlantic species by its yellow and black body edged with scarlet, and the slightly elongated rays of the dorsal and anal fins. You have to search carefully for the Rock Beauty; being a "loner," it rarely ventures far from its protective abode.

Various species of Angelfishes are found in tropical and subtropical waters the world over.

THE BUTTERFLY FISHES—FAMILY *CHAETODONTIDAE*

Although of the same family as the Angelfishes, the Butterfly Fishes are usually divided into a separate group. They are much smaller than the Angelfishes, maturing at a length of six to eight inches. The extended snouts of these fishes enable them to reach into cracks and crevices of the coral for plant food and small invertebrates upon which they feed.

Active little fishes, they are usually seen in pairs, flitting about from coral head to coral head "butterfly fashion," which is probably how they acquired their name. These pretty small fishes are found on tropical reefs all over the world and are valued by fish collectors everywhere. One of the most brilliantly colored is the orange-striped Long Nose Butterfly (*Chelmon rostratus*) found in tropical Indo-Pacific waters from northern Australia to Mauritius. Indeed, there are many similar species in this region and all are extremely brightly colored.

The Four-eyed Butterfly Fish (*Chaetodon capistratus*) derives its name from the large false eye located near the tail. This confuses its many predators and enables the Butterfly Fish to flit swiftly away in what appears to be a backward direction. Sharp spines on the back of the Butterfly make an unpleasant mouthful and afford him dual protection.

The Four-eyed Butterfly Fish in the photo on the opposite page has an isopod clinging beneath its real eye. These isopods belong to a well-known group of crustaceans and can be either predatory or parasitic.

The Common Butterfly Fish (*Chaetodon ocellatus*) has a whitish body with a bright yellow fin and tail and a dark band through the eye. The base of the dorsal fin sometimes has a large dark spot. Common in West Indian waters, it has been known to stray as far north as Massachusetts.

The exceedingly pretty Banded Butterfly Fish (*Chaetodon striatus*) is fortunately quite common and dresses up the coral reef with its trim black-and-white striped body.

Some Butterfly Fishes have been observed acting as "cleaner fishes" for other species. Their small buck teeth are suited for this purpose. Butterfly Fishes will be frequent companions on many of your snorkeling trips, but they are active and alert so don't count on getting too close.

The Banded Butterfly Fish will be a frequent companion on many of your snorkeling promenades.

The false eye of the Four-eyed Butterfly Fish is a distracting lure for predators. Here, a parasite has attached itself under the real eye. (See bottom picture, page 44.)

THE SNAPPERS—FAMILY *LUTIANIDAE*

The Yellow-tail Snapper (*Ocyurus chrysurus*), a handsome member of the Snapper family has yellow fins and a yellow stripe along its blue body, the upper half of which has yellow spots. Growing to about two feet, the Yellow-tail has a reputation as a good eating fish and is much sought after by spearfishermen. Unlike most Snappers which are often found in schools, the Yellow-tail is frequently found alone among the waving arms of soft Sea Whips. Speedy and wary as are most Snappers, the Yellow-tail is usually difficult to photograph.

A Yellow-tail Snapper swims towards the soft, waving arms of Sea Whip Coral.

While the Yellow-tails can usually be found near reefs, it is not uncommon to see them swimming over a wide variety of mud, sand, or grass bottoms. The Yellow-tail doesn't seem to follow the usual Snapper haunts of dark areas and ledges.

A similar American West Coast species, the Rabirubia (*Rabirubia inermis*) is similar in shape to the Yellow-tail, but this Snapper is rose-colored and only reaches one foot in length.

The three Mutton-fish (*Lutianus analis*) pictured below are also members of the Snapper family. This species can attain 25 pounds, though is more commonly between eight and ten pounds. The prominent blue bar under the eye provides fairly easy identification for the Mutton-fish. It does look very much like the Gray Snapper (*Lutianus griseus*), except for the red fins that the Mutton-fish displays. The fiery red eye of the Mutton-fish also aids in identifying this West Indian fish.

Several other members of this family are similar to the Mutton-fish and Gray Snapper. The Dog Snapper (*Lutianus*

A trio of Mutton-fish swim in formation.

jocu) has been seen as far north as Cape Cod. This fish displays a great deal of red and copperish coloring and may reach a weight of 20 pounds.

A species similar to those described is another Dog Snapper (*Lutianus novemfasciatus*), who resembles the Gray Snapper in body color when young, but takes on a more reddish-brown coloring as he matures. This Snapper is seen as far south as Panama. The presence of large canine teeth probably accounts

Schoolmaster Snappers, sometimes found lurking under ledges in typical snapper fashion, here swim past the camera at 65 feet.

The branches of Elkhorn Coral and Finger Coral shelter a group of Schoolmaster Snappers in their shallow retreat.

for the Dog Snapper's name. Common names are frequently misleading, as these are generally names which have been given as a description of a particular fish's appearance or habits, plus the fact that these common names vary from one geographic area to another.

The Schoolmaster Snapper (*Lutianus apodus*) is a commonly seen Snapper in southern Atlantic and Caribbean waters. The body color varies, but a distinctive feature of this popular species is that it is the only Snapper whose fins are all-over yellowish. Young Schoolmasters have also been known as far north as Cape Cod. The blue bar below the eye identifies these young species from other members of the Snapper family. Spearfishermen have found the larger Schoolmasters lurking, in typical Snapper fashion, under deep ledges. They are typically nervous and shy away at the first demonstration of aggression, and for this reason they are one of the most difficult fishes to photograph. One technique frequently used by spearfishermen, as well as the underwater hunter armed with a camera, is to dive to the bottom and remain motionless. You can usually steady yourself by holding on to a rock or coral head. Once the Snapper spots you, he will approach cautiously. This technique can be practiced over and over with the same fish until you finally get your "shot."

Another species found in southern Mexico, also called a Yellow-tail, strongly resembles the Schoolmaster—except that this Snapper (*Lutianus argentiventris*) is rosy on the front part of the body and more yellow towards the rear.

Probably the best known is the Red Snapper (*Lutianus aya*), usually found in deep waters. This species is a delicious food fish and is found from Florida north to South Carolina. The anal and soft dorsal fins of this fish easily distinguish it from other Snappers of similar appearance, because these fins are angular rather than rounded as in the other species. Coloring is rose-red, though this is not uncommon among Snappers. A similar fish is the West Indian Silk Snapper (*Lutianus vivanus*). This last species grows to 40 pounds, and has a yellow tail and red body.

THE SEA BASSES—FAMILY *SERRANIDAE*

Perhaps the best known members of this family are the Groupers and the large Sea Basses—commonly called Jewfish. This is a widely diversified family found the world over in warm temperate and tropical seas and comprising many important food fishes. The size and range is extraordinary—the Butter Hamlet (*Hypoplecturus unicolor*) grows to a length of less than one foot, while the Black Jewfish (*Garrupa nigrita*) is known to reach a length of six feet and a weight of close to 500 pounds.

Basses are usually "homing" fish and stay close to their caves or rocky retreats. If they have not been frightened by local spearfishermen you may be able to become quite friendly with some Groupers by chumming them. They are extremely curious and after getting to know you will readily follow you about. Perhaps the most familiar Grouper was Ulysses, whom Jacques Cousteau's diving activities made famous. After befriending the divers Ulysses made such a nuisance of himself following the Cousteau team around that he had to be put in a cage.

The Queensland Grouper (*Promicrops lanceolatus*), a related Australian species, is the largest known Grouper. It is said to

Sporting a parasite under each eye, this Rock Hind peers out from beneath a stump of Staghorn Coral.

In a Mediterranean grotto, schooling Sea Basses peer cautiously out
at the intruding camera.

Camouflaged among corals and sponges, a Red Hind awaits its unsuspecting prey.

grow as long as 12 feet and to weigh close to 1,000 pounds. Its disconcerting habit of following divers "cat-and-mouse" fashion sometimes makes divers more wary of this fish than of sharks.

One of the small West Indian members of the Grouper family, the Rock Hind (*Epinephelus adscensions*), has small red-brown spots covering its entire body. Look for these small Groupers under coral ledges and tucked in rocky crevices. Another similar species, the Red Hind (*Epinephelus guttatus*), has the same coloring but its dorsal, tail, and anal fins are strikingly edged in black. The Spotted Cabrilla (*Epinephelus analogus*), also related to the Rock Hind, is a member of an abundant California species. The Sea Bass (*Anthias anthias*) is a common

A Butter Hamlet, a member of the Grouper family, hangs suspended in its coral jungle.

coastal species of the Mediterranean Sea and along the tropical and warm temperate parts of the Atlantic coast of Africa.

The several color phases of the Coney (*Cephalopholis fulvus*), a common West Indian species, make identification tricky— look for the black-tipped jaws and the two dark spots near the base of its tail. You will have to look carefully, too, for the Graysby (*Petrometopon cruentatus*) for, although common, this fish adapts itself well to its underwater surroundings and is difficult to see.

Protective coloration aids the Graysby (below) in hiding from
predators.

Brown on top, cream on bottom, this Coney seeks shelter under a
ledge of coral. Spiny Sea Urchins cover reef bottoms almost everywhere.

Blue-striped Grunts, commonly found in tropical waters, nestle under branches of Elkhorn Coral.

THE GRUNTS—FAMILY *HAEMULIDAE*

Common to tropical waters, the Grunts are handsome little fishes closely related to the Snappers. They receive their name from the grunting sounds they are capable of producing—especially when they are removed from the water. Usually schooling in habits, large groups of Grunts swarm around coral heads.

You will also see the Caesar (*Bathystoma rimator*), a shallow water inhabitant, swimming about the coral heads, nosing into every crack and cranny in its diligent search for food. They feed mostly on invertebrates and have been known to annoy offshore fishermen by constantly nibbling at bait intended for larger fish. You can recognize the Caesar by its silver-grey color and two prominent yellow lines, one from the eye to the tail, and one above that from the head to the end of the dorsal fin. Young Caesars have horizontal dark lines and a dark caudal spot.

The high forehead and distinctive markings of the Porkfish

Tightly-grouped Yellow-striped Grunts surround a growth of Fire Coral.

A Margate (right) is surprised by the appearance of a Bermuda Chub who has discovered its coral refuge. The Margate is often mistaken for a snapper.

(*Anisotremus virginicus*) make it a striking member of the Grunt family. They travel singly as often as in dense schools. A close relative of the Porkfish is the Sargo (*Anisotremus davidsoni*), a rather drab fish by comparison. Dull silvery-grey in color, this species is the only Grunt found in the Southern California coastal waters.

The Blue-striped Grunt (*Haemulon sciurus*) is famous for its "kissing" activities. This is a peculiar habit they have of rushing at one another open mouthed and "kissing." The reason for this strange conduct has not yet been determined, but it is

Young Caesar Grunts mill aimlessly over beds of Star Coral.

thought to be either a display of territorial aggressiveness or courtship activity. Other species of Grunts have also been observed demonstrating in this same manner.

The habits of the Yellow Grunt (*Haemulon flavolineatum*) are very similar to those of the Blue-striped species. These little Grunts are noted for their sunny shadow-striped yellow bodies that match their colorful surroundings. Like most Grunts they have large glassy eyes, and the insides of their mouths are vivid red.

A relatively large fish, the Margate (*Haemulon albium*) is valued as a good eating fish, and is often mistaken for a Snapper. The pearly-grey Margate leads a solitary life off the deeper waters of the coral reef. The spawning time is early summer at which time this fish schools. The Black Margate (*Anisotremus surinamensis*) reaches a larger size than any of the other Grunts and is much sought by spearfishermen.

A Porkfish (top) is about to encounter a Squirrel Fish (bottom).

Frequently found in Mediterranean grottoes are Breams.

THE PORGIES and SEA BREAMS—FAMILY *SPARIDAE*

Porgies, small-mouthed fish equipped with strong incisor teeth, feed on shellfish, invertebrates and small fishes. Most Porgies are identified by a high back and compressed body.

There are a number of species of Porgies or Sea Breams in the Mediterranean and off the north European coast. English fishermen trawl for the Common Sea Bream (*Pagellus centradontus*) in deep waters. The Red Porgy (*Pagrus pagrus*) is a southern European species sometimes found off the coast of Florida.

Porgies are abundant from the West Indies to the Florida Keys. Usually found in deeper waters over a sandy or grass bottom, the Porgies are very nervous and extremely difficult to approach.

The Saucer-eye Porgy (*Calamus calamus*) receives its name from its large yellow saucer-like eyes. Quite common in the West Indies, it reaches a length of about 15 inches. By far the most common of the Porgies is the Jolt-head Porgy (*Calamus bajonado*), purported to have earned its name from its habit of jolting molluscs loose from rocks with its jaws.

Gobies flit in front of a Queen Angelfish. The little fishes are often seen clinging to coral.

A Saucer-eye Porgy, a common inhabitant of tropical waters, is trailed by a Yellow-striped Goatfish.

THE CRUSTACEANS

The Slipper Lobster (*Parribaccus antarcticus*), unlike its spiny cousins, hides itself, head-first, in a coral head with its tail exposed. The Slipper Lobster does not have his cousins' long spiny antennae, so he relies on his adaptive coloring and rock-like appearance for protection. The Slipper Lobster's Mediterranean counterpart is the "Cigale," well known to divers.

The Spiny Lobster (*Panulirus argus*) is found in protected crevices and small openings on the rocky bottom. The Spiny Lobster will peer at you from the opening of his cave with his antennae waving and as soon as he detects your approach he

Rarely seen in full view, the Slipper Lobster is as tasty as its spiny cousins.

will retreat to the back of the cave. The California variety of Spiny Lobsters (*Panulirus interruptus*) are referred to as "bugs," and there is a strictly controlled season for capturing them. Legally, they can only be taken by hand.

Another species of Spiny Lobster (*Panulirus vulgaris*) is abundant on the southern and western shores of England.

The Arrow Crab (*Stenorhychus*), much like a celebrity from the entertainment world, is named for the shape of its nose. Slow moving, it depends on its concealing shape for protection.

Careful searching around rocks and coral heads will produce

Often sharing its home with a Moray Eel, the Spiny Lobster is much sought after by divers.

The Arrow Crab is another slow-moving mariner that must depend upon its concealing shape for protection.

White antennae often reveal the hideout of a Banded Coral Shrimp.

such interesting specimens as the Banded Coral Shrimp (*Stenopus hispidus*). Their lengthy white antennae are easily spotted and if gently pulled, will bring the little shrimp out. This shrimp is a parasite cleaner and even enters the mouths of Moray Eels to pick parasites from their jaws.

REEF FISH—FAMILY *POMACENTRIDAE*

Easily identified by its black-edged swallowtail, the Reef Fish (*Chromis marginatus*) is one of the most abundant of all the members of the reef. Belonging to the Demoiselle family, the Reef Fish is usually found in large numbers swarming around coral heads. It has two color phases—light brown and bright blue. A related American West Coast species is the Blacksmith (*Ayresia punctipinnis*).

Above, a Reef Fish in its brown phase hovers over a large Basket Sponge. Below, the forked tail and bright blue color are distinctive features of the other color phase of this fish. A Four-eyed Butterfly Fish swims below.

A lone Blue Tang accompanies its Doctorfish cousins.

Only a camera can capture and preserve a scene such as this. The dozens of Doctorfishes convening along this reef were undisturbed by the presence of the photographer.

THE SURGEONFISHES—FAMILY *ACANTHURIDAE*

The Doctorfishes (*Acanthurus hepatus*) derive their professional-sounding name from the scalpel-like device on each side of their tails. This lance-like spine, when erected, enables the fish to inflict deep gashes by "sideswiping" its adversary. (The peaceable, plant-eating Doctorfish will snap open its sharp spines in emergencies, and often scars the hands of unknowing fishermen.)

Various shades of brown in color, Doctorfishes school densely around the coral reef. A West Indian species, they have been known to stray as far north as New York. Many colorful species of Surgeonfish are found throughout the Pacific

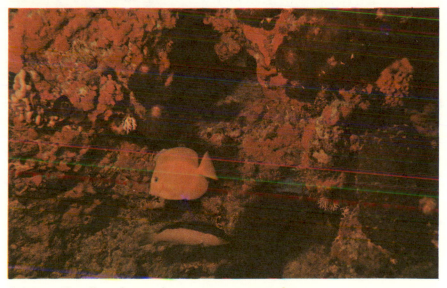

A young Blue Tang hovers in a sponge-encrusted cave.

from southern Japan to Australia, to the Philippines and Hawaii.

The constantly "smiling" Blue Tangs (*Acanthurus caeruleus*) are usually seen following the Doctorfishes around the reef. Closely related to the Doctorfish, the Blue Tang also has a knifelike spine near the tail. The young Blue Tang are a bright yellow and change gradually to bright blue as they mature. At night the Blue Tang changes its colors once again. Its bright blue body becomes striped with greyish bands making it look like a totally different species.

THE SQUIRREL FISHES—FAMILY *HOLOCENTRIDAE*

During the day these timid little fishes are hard to find, because they stay holed up in their caves. Even with their bright colorings it is difficult to see them, as they rarely venture outside the coral crevices of their homes. They are, however, quite common reef-fish and as your eyes become more trained in searching the underwater world you will see many Squirrel Fishes. Look for a pinkish to red body (the color varies), large, dark protruding eyes, and sharp, whitish spines. As their large eyes indicate, these fishes have nocturnal habits. At night they venture from their coral retreats out on to the reef, foraging for the small fishes and crustaceans upon which they feed. The Longspine Squirrel Fish (*Holocentrus rufus*) is a common tropical Atlantic species. There are many related species found in the tropical Pacific.

THE BIG-EYES—FAMILY *PRIACANTHIDAE*

The deep red Common Big-Eye (*Priacanthus arenatus*) derives its name from its large glassy eyes. Sometimes confused with the Squirrel Fish, the Big-Eye is found in much deeper waters and does not have long spines on its back. Another member of this family is the Deep Big-Eye (*Pseudopriacanthus altus*). Its brilliant red coloring and deep, almost round, body identifies this fish. Although widely distributed, there are fewer than twenty-four recognized species of this family.

THE CARDINAL FISHES—FAMILY *CHEILODIPTERIDAE*

A large-eyed red Cardinal Fish is the Conchfish (*Apogonichthys stellatus*). This fish, maturing at a length of 2 inches, is often found hiding in the hollows of large shells, notably the conchs from where it gets its name. Conchfishes apparently use the conchs for shelter only, as they feed mostly on small invertebrates. They are also known to use the cavities of sponges for the same purpose.

The Cardinal Fishes are tropical water species and are found in tropical Atlantic and Indo-Pacific waters.

Squirrel Fishes are usually found in dark places where their brilliant color is less revealing.

The Common Big-Eye is often mistaken for the Squirrel Fish, but has much shorter fins.

The Longspine Squirrel Fish is rarely seen in the open during the day.

THE TRUMPET FISHES—FAMILY *AULOSTOMIDAE*

The Trumpet Fish (*Aulostomus maculatus*) seems to float rather than swim among the coral heads. Never in a hurry, the bizarre Trumpet Fish is often seen standing on its head among the soft coral Sea Whips, imitating the Sea Whips and surveying the scene with its cold flat eyes. Usually mottled light brown in color, the Trumpet Fish is quite difficult to see against a coral and rock background. Although some bright yellow species have been seen, they are not common.

THE TRUNKFISHES—FAMILY *OSTRACIIDAE*

A poor swimmer, the Trunkfish (*Lactophrys trigonus*) depends on its hard solid shell, which covers almost its entire body, for protection. Flapping its tiny dorsal and anal fins, the Trunkfish finds it difficult to propel its rigid body through the water

Can you spot the Trumpet Fish camouflaged among the swaying Sea Whips?

Here, the Trumpet Fish is undisturbed and travels in full view.

The Common Trunkfish is speckled like its coral background.

The Cowfish, with its odd shape, assumes an iridescent color when frightened.

swiftly. Although small, Trunkfishes are considered good eating and are often baked or roasted in their shells.

The box-like Cowfish (*Lactophrys tricornis*) is a colorful member of the Trunkfish family. Like the Common Trunkfish, only the eyes, mouth and fins protrude from its protective shell, making it an awkward and vulnerable swimmer. The Cowfish has two strong spines over the eyes that are directed forward, and it is a blotchy blue-green and yellow in color. When badly frightened these colors are intensified, the blue becoming especially iridescent.

The Shellfish is so-called because of its hard shell-like exterior. It has counter-rotating fins.

The Shellfish (*Lactophrys bicaudalis*) is a rarer and more valued species of the Trunkfishes. It has a spine just ahead of the anal fin, pointing backwards, and its color is grey with dark round spots.

Trunkfishes are common to most tropical seas.

The little fish on the underbelly of this Nurse Shark is a Remora—a free rider who feasts on the crumbs of its host's meal.

CARTILAGINOUS CREATURES

The Nurse Shark (*Ginglymostoma cirratum*) is a sluggish and usually inoffensive animal. However, it is often abused, even by divers who know the extent of its temper when aroused, and there have been a number of cases of divers being bitten by this shark. Although not equipped with large teeth as are most sharks, the Nurse Shark does grow to about 14 feet in length and should be left alone!

You might occasionally see a Remora (*Echeneis naucrates*) attached to sharks or other large fishes. When the "host" is feeding, the Remora loosens its suction-like hold and scavenges around on its own. If you allowed him, the Remora would travel happily along on *you*.

The Say's Sting Ray (*Dasyatis say*) is most commonly found lying motionless on the sea-floor, nearly invisible. Rays are bottom-feeders, catching small shrimps and crabs which emerge from the sand, and using their pectoral fins to dig for shells buried in the sand.

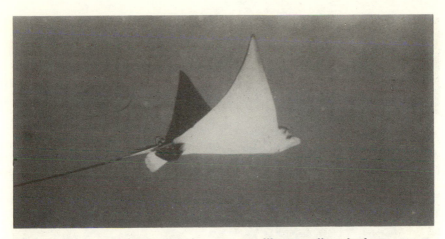

Like a bird the Eagle Ray wings its way speedily, revealing the horny
barb at the base of its tail.

The Spotted Eagle Ray (*Aëtobatus narinari*) is a spectacular
looking Ray, beautiful and non-aggressive. It feeds mostly
on hard-shelled molluscs, using its powerful jaws to crush the
thick shells.

Though not aggressive, the Sting Ray does possess a formidable weapon
—its serrated tail-spine.

These two Snakefishes are tireless hunters ready to pounce upon unsuspecting prey.

No beauty contest winner is the Scorpion Fish. Stay away from this spiny denizen of the Mediterranean deep.

THE BOTTOM DWELLERS

When searching for Octopuses, look for a pile of shells and rocks, as this might indicate that an Octopus is living nearby. He feeds mostly on small crustaceans, such as crabs, which he will snatch from the rear, holding their pincers away with his tentacles while he injects a poison with his small but powerful beak. A master of camouflage, he is able to turn any shade or pattern to match his surroundings.

Blending in with the sandy or coral bottom, the Snakefish (*Trachinocephalus myops*) is almost impossible to spot. He lies absolutely motionless, even when approached quite closely, and

The Octopus is capable of changing color to blend into its environment.

awaits his prey. The California Lizard Fish (*Synodus lucioceps*) is very closely related to the above species.

The Scorpion Fish (*Scorpaena porcus*), or "rascasse" as it is sometimes known, is a rather repulsive creature of the Mediterranean Sea. Closely related species are found the world over including the deadly Stone Fish (*Synanceja horrida*) of the South Pacific, the Lionfish (*Scorpaena grandicornis*) of the West Indies, and the California Scorpion Fish (*Scorpaena guttata*).

Usually seen in groups of two or three, Squid swim as though jet-propelled.

SQUID—*CEPHALOPODA*

The bright-eyed small Squid are often seen swimming in precise formations near the surface of warm tropical waters. Retiring little fellows, these Squid (*Sepioteuthis sepiodea*) are not at all like the terrible stories written about them. Squid are found the world over from the Little Squid (*Sepiola atlantica*), common on the coasts of Britain, to the Giant Squid, a deep-water inhabitant of the South American coastal waters. Squid are one of the speediest of marine animals, propelled along as water is drawn in, then forcibly ejected.

THE PORCUPINE FISHES—FAMILY *DIDONTIDAE*

The slow-moving Porcupine Fish (*Diodon hystrix*) has one of the most effective protective devices of all the fishes. When in danger, it inflates its body into a round ball and erects all its long quill-like appendages into a formidable bulwark. The American West Coast Boxfish (*Chilomycterus affinis*) is a related species.

The tiny Sharp-nosed Puffer (*Canthigaster rostratus*) belongs to a similar species, the Swellfishes of the family *Tetraodontidae*. Rarely larger than four inches long, it makes its home among the Sea Fans and other Gorgonians.

The tiny Sharp-nosed Puffer flits among the swaying soft Gorgonians.

The Porcupine Fish is rarely seen outside its coral home where its color blends with the surroundings.

Unlike ostriches, Garden Eels raise their heads from the sand, in which they make their home. They feed on plankton.

The Moray Eel is potentially dangerous if molested. Keep your hands away from holes in the reef where it might be lurking.

BOTTOM FEEDERS

Looking, in groups, like a meadow of waving grass, Garden Eels (*Troglodyte eel*) have adopted a plantlike way of life: you might witness a feeding ritual if you approach them carefully. Stretching a foot or more from their homes in the sand, they will snatch planktonic food from the water. Similar species have been found in California and the Indian Ocean.

Seldom seen out in the open, the Ribbon Fish (*Eques acuminatus*) prefers to stay close to caves and hiding places along the reef. It is timid and therefore difficult to study. Never still for a second, it is always twisting and turning its oddly striped

Seldom seen by snorkelers, the Ribbon Fish is a tempting catch for the fish collector.

body. It has three main stripes: from the dorsal to the tail, from the head to the pectoral, and one across the eye.

The Spotted Moray (*Gymnothorax moringa*), a sinister-looking character, spends his time lurking in deep coral crevasses. Not known to deliberately attack skin divers, he does defend his lair with evil aggressiveness. The European habit of poking in holes with bare hands is a dangerous trick in tropical waters! A similar species, the Californian Moray (*Gymnothorax mordax*) has almost the same coloring and markings as the West Indian Spotted Moray.

THE DEMOISELLES—FAMILY *POMACENTRIDAE*

Among the most beautiful of reef dwellers are the Demoiselles. The young are often dotted with shining blue spots as brilliant as jewels. Harmlessly aggressive, these tiny fishes are distributed in all tropical seas.

The Beau Gregory (*Pomacentrus leucostictus*), commonly seen among the swarms of reef-fish, has many different color phases. It has been seen in various shades of brown, blue, and yellow, and even with iridescent blue spots. Known to the West Indies and West Coast of Mexico, the Beau Gregory's many varied colorings make it exceedingly difficult to identify accurately.

Perhaps the most common of the reef-inhabitants is the Sergeant-Major (*Abudef saxatilis*), a vigilant fish that rarely rests. A curious little fellow, the Sergeant-Major is easily chummed and always a willing subject to photograph. It spends most of its time driving away the Wrasses and other fishes that eat its eggs at every opportunity. This fish is known on both sides of the Atlantic as well as the Pacific.

The bright-orange Garibaldi (*Hypsypops rubicunda*), inhabitant of the kelp beds of Southern California, is also a member of the Demoiselle family.

Most common of the reef fishes are the popular Sergeant-Majors, seen here huddled in a hollow of Finger Coral.

Beau Gregory swims precariously above the sharp spines of the Sea
Urchins.

A Demoiselle seems suspended before lovely patches of Red Sponge.

Skip Jacks are masters of camouflage.

SCHOOLING FISHES

Camouflage plays an important part in the life of the Skip Jack (*Caranx ruber*). Enemies from above find it hard to distinguish their blue backs from the surrounding water. From below, their light undersides blend into the bright sky. Skip Jacks are often seen following a barracuda, hoping to share in the crumbs from its table. There are many, many species of Jacks all over the world.

Masses of Glassy Sweepers (*Pempheris schomburgki*) are seen moving together in waves under dark ledges of coral. Very little is known about this uncommon fish.

You may see the Houndfish (*Strongylura raphidoma*) taking to the air in repeated leaps and hurdling objects, apparently just for the sport of it. The Houndfish reaches a length of over four feet and has been known to jump into and over small fishing boats in the tropics, accidentally injuring fishermen with its spearlike beak. A widely distributed species, it is known in the Mediterranean as well as in the Atlantic.

The silvery little fishes sometimes seen schooling densely, close to shore, are the reef Silversides (*Allanetta*).

90

Glassy Sweepers move in waves through dark caverns.

A Houndfish, surrounded by little Silversides, drifts along just below the surface.

The Queen Triggerfish, perhaps the most beautiful member of the family, extends the trigger on top of its head when threatened.

The Orange Filefish also has a protective trigger on the top of its head.

THE TRIGGERFISHES—FAMILY *BALISTIDAE*

Triggerfishes are a shallow-water, tropical species. Rather slow-moving in their habits, these Triggerfishes are usually solitary swimmers. Of the thirty species of Triggerfishes, none exceeds about 2 feet in length.

These fishes receive their name from the locking mechanism of the spines of the first and second dorsal fins. When the large first dorsal spine locks erect into place, the small third spine must be depressed before the first will relax.

One of the largest Triggerfishes, the Ocean Triggerfish (*Canthidermis sabaco*) reaches a length of 2 feet and is dark grey in color. This Triggerfish is common in the West Indies, though it has been found as far north as New York.

The Queen Triggerfish (*Balistes vetula*) will often be seen swimming off the hard bottom near the reef. This fish is capable of rapid color change, depending upon the degree of lightness or darkness of the bottom. Being a good eating fish, the Queen, or "oldwife," as she is often called in the West Indies, is popular among spearfishermen. The tough, leathery skin can be removed in one piece and used as a crude form of sandpaper.

The Pacific Triggerfish (*Verrunculus polylepis*) is a related species found off the California coast. This fish varies from dark to light brown in color and grows to 2 feet.

THE FILEFISHES—FAMILY *MONOCANTHIDAE*

The Orange Filefish (*Alutera schoepfi*) is closely related to the Triggerfishes. Filefishes also have a dorsal spine, but not the trigger-like arrangement of their cousins. The Orange Filefish is a rather awkward but handsomely marked fish that is often seen poking around coral heads, crunching on small plants and animals. He is sometimes seen hanging motionless, head down.

Filefishes are found world-wide in tropical waters, though some, like the Common Filefish (*Monacanthus hispidus*), are found as far north as Maine. This little Filefish reaches about 10 inches.

One of the largest members of this family, the Scrawled Filefish (*Alutera scripta*) reaches three feet in length, and is found in tropical seas around the world. Being a very curious fish, the Scrawled Filefish will often swim slowly around you until it seems well satisfied. This, however, may take several minutes!

THE WALLFISH

The lovely Royal Gramma (*Gramma hemichrysos*), actually belonging to the Sea Basses (*Serranidae*), will be found under dark ledges and in caverns, living an upside-down life. The exotic purple and gold coloration of the Royal Gramma is unmistakable. Its darting movements make close study of this fish difficult, and photography even more so.

ODDITIES

The sausage-shaped Sea-Cucumber (*Holothuria floridana*), Trepang or Bêche-de-mer ("Sea-Slug" or "Sea-Worm") is aptly named. Like the earthworm, the chartreuse-tinted Sea-Cucumber continually swallows mud and sand from which it extracts organic matter. When irritated, a Sea-Cucumber ejects sticky strands; irritated further, it might even throw out all its internal organs, only to grow a new set within a matter of days.

Upon closer investigation, you might discover a Pearlfish (*Carapus bermudensis*) living inside the Sea-Cucumber. In the Pacific, these little fishes sometimes inhabit pearl oysters and starfishes.

The purple Royal Gramma swim upside-down and make their home up against the sponge-encrusted wall.

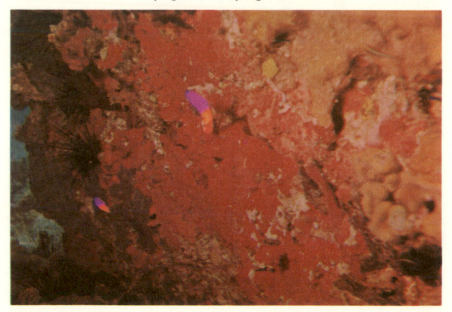

The Sea-Cucumber, shown here, has a built-in protection against marine predators.

The sluggish Sea-Cucumber, like other bottom dwellers such as the Starfish and Sea Urchin, creeps slowly along the bottom. Ranging up to three feet in length, the leathery-skinned creatures crawl along by body contractions, using their tiny tube-feet, which are like those of their Starfish relatives.

The Flame Scallop (*Pectinidae*) is one of the collector's prize shells. These Scallops are surprisingly good swimmers. As their valve opens, the inner space fills with water, a powerful muscle contracts, and the valve pulls shut, shooting the water out behind and sending the little mollusc forward. Look for these beautiful Flame Scallops in narrow crevices off the rocky and coral bottom.

You will find the Peacock Flounder (*Platophrys lunatus*) on the sandy bottom near the reef, but you will have to look sharply to spot him as he is provided with excellent concealing colorations. Very often, Flounders cover themselves with sand and remain motionless. The light-blue circles covering the Peacock make identification easy. Common to the tropics, it has been seen from New York to Brazil.

A Flame Scallop nestles in its coral home next to a spiny black Sea Urchin.

A Peacock Flounder scurries across the sandy bottom.

HAZARDOUS MARINE LIFE

Sea Urchins are probably responsible for more diving mishaps than any other marine animal. If the diver should accidentally step on an Urchin or bump against one, the barbed spines will puncture the skin and usually break off. Although, if left alone, these spines will be absorbed by the skin, a 10 per cent by volume concentration of hydrogen peroxide aids in dissolving them.

In some places, for example in southern California, seaweed (kelp) often spreads a canopy-like covering over the water's surface. Though this is often an ideal environment for diving because it provides an abundance of many forms of marine life, it can also be disconcerting to a diver returning from a deep dive. In such a situation, the diver should keep his hands extended over his head as he nears the surface, parting the kelp when he reaches the top. A diver who becomes entangled should use his knife to cut through the thin branches. Working slowly will prevent further entanglement.

Sting Rays are not aggressive animals, but can inflict a painful wound if stepped on accidentally. Use a shuffling motion of the feet when entering shallow-water areas known to be frequented by Rays.

Eels, Morays and Congers are another hazard to the diver who "pokes" around holes and crevices. Not known to be aggressive, eels *will* bite if threatened or provoked. Incidentally, if you are taking lobsters by "snare" or hand and notice that one antenna is pointing to the side, towards a source of potential danger, you can bet that an eel is sharing the same lair!

There is a great deal of controversy on the danger of sharks. The best advice is to leave the water if large sharks are present. If this is not possible, remain calm, swim towards the boat or shore in an easy manner without undue splashing, keeping the shark within sight at all times. It is wise to remember to always stay close to your swimming companion.

Barracuda have a habit of appearing suddenly and will usually disappear in the same manner; they are very curious and will sometimes follow the reef-snorkeler for a great distance. Though their gruesome appearance might be alarming, there is no need to leave the water unless the barracuda seems to be swimming in a quick, agitated manner.

FISH AND CORAL COLLECTING

Collection for scientific study or hobby is quite different from spearfishing, wreck-diving, or even photography, but can be equally exciting and challenging.

If you have spent many hours underwater observing marine creatures in their various shallow-water habitats, spearing fish, exploring wrecks, and even searching for treasure, perhaps you have recorded some of the activity patterns and reactions of different forms of undersea life. If so, collection will be that much easier. Use this book to identify common reef-dwellers, making a systematic study of those you might wish to collect and preserve. Begin to observe how fishes live and you will discover there is much of interest and importance which is not yet recorded—which can only be learned as you have done, by observing marine life in its natural environment. As you can see from the picture on the opposite page, approaching small fishes can be accomplished easily if not done in a threatening manner.

Making a collection of small fresh-water and salt-water fishes and animals can be as easy and gratifying as collecting shells—and, perhaps, more exciting! But take the time to develop the necessary skills and learn to work safely and unhurriedly to get the best results.

An important consideration in your bid at collecting is knowledge of the areas where you will hunt specimens. Living along the southern Atlantic coast provides an excellent opportunity to work in true aquarium-fish waters. Generally speaking, the warmer the water, the more brilliant the fish; however, some of the loveliest varieties of aquarium fishes come from the Pacific West Coast. There you will find such fishes as the Garibaldi, Catalina Goby, and even the prized Mantis Shrimp.

The fishes you've been diving among have been salt-water species—which have become an important specialty within the collector's world. But the backbone of the aquarium industry has always been the fresh-water collectors. In either

Move in silently when using a slurp-gun—sudden movements frighten fish.

The diver's knife is not intended for defence, but is useful for prying purposes or occasional cutting of lines.

case, however, the hunting, capturing and transporting techniques are approximately the same.

As in spearfishing, knowing where to seek the sea creatures is half the game; and the chances are that if you return to the same areas where your speargun was king, you'll now find the "little game" in the same haunts. The rocks, crevices, caves, coral jungles, and kelp beds are the best spots to begin.

Continue with your basic snorkeling equipment, but add a net, "slurp-gun," and glass jars for collecting smaller specimens. Be sure to have your knife along to chop up Sea Urchins for chumming, and for prying any fragments from the coral. You might try anaesthetizing some free-swimming fishes. There are chemicals available which can be sprayed directly into the gills,

A float provides a useful base of operations while collecting specimens.

taking effect instantly. An ideal underwater syringe for this purpose is a plastic squeeze-bottle.

If you intend to transport live specimens, plastic containers will be required, as metal receptacles can poison the fish. Have a bucket on hand to carry starfishes and other fairly large creatures.

For many years the typical collector of tropical fishes would spend most of his collecting day armed only with a net and wide-mouth gallon jar. If, by the end of the day, he happened to have four or five specimens to his credit, the day was a complete success.

Today, however, with the advent of the slurp-gun (a vacuum-type plastic gun that inhales fish rather than firing something at them), the modern collector can easily capture dozens of small marine creatures in an afternoon. Once you have located the fish you want, and have either got him "holed-up," or feeding from a Sea Urchin or other chum you're using, dive down, place the muzzle of the gun next to the hole or near the bait, pull the trigger and watch as the little fish is quickly ingested into the barrel.

Some slurp-guns allow the user to "blow" a little water out of the gun towards the fish. These operate on the principle that most smaller fishes are conditioned to a change in the current between themselves and a larger predator who is feeding. When they feel the sucking action of his inhalation, they simply swim the opposite way—*if* they are quick enough. Often the fishes will swim directly into the muzzle after feeling the blowing sensation of the gun.

Once safely taken, a piston gently forces the fish into a holding chamber, and you are ready to dive again. While in the holding chamber of the slurp-gun, the fish is actually acting as a decoy for the next specimen.

Slurp-gunning, like any new technique, takes practice and with a little experience the slurp-gun will prove a valuable tool in your collecting.

You may have to revert to anæsthetizing agents for some of the fishes which hide in small holes or crevices. One particular

Take care when poking around holes—eels frequently lurk inside them.

The taking of female lobsters is generally forbidden. Note the red eggs beneath the tail.

Employing this "snare" is the sporting way to catch lobsters.

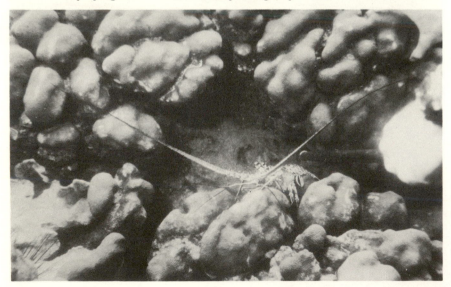

drug, quinaldine, can be squirted into the holes where small fishes are hiding. Then you can easily capture the specimens with your net as they emerge from their shelter. For best results with small fishes and amphibians, use an inch of concentrated acetone solution of the anæsthetic in a plastic bottle, and then fill to the top with sea water. Quinaldine is extremely irritating if it comes in contact with the skin, so use it carefully.

One of the most widely used techniques for capturing live fish specimens involves the use of dip nets. Take two small dip nets, one in each hand. Dive and trap your fish and bring him to the surface with the mouth of the net held upward. When a fish is moved away from the bottom, it expends all its energy fighting to go downward, so there is no need to cover the net. As soon as you have swept for the fish, direct the mouth of the net upward.

Another interesting method is using a dip net and a glass or other transparent jar. Approach the fish with the net and frighten him into the jar. The fish will be fooled by the transparent jar and he won't realize he is entering a one-way street!

Many small fishes can be baited easily by simply crushing Sea Urchins and placing them in an empty bottle on the bottom. As soon as a small fish has entered the bottle to feed—on goes the lid.

Traps provide another excellent method for the capture of swimming specimens. Though fish-pots and traps come in various sizes and shapes, the fundamental principle common to all is in the conical section that leads towards the middle. Usually there is a small vertical opening, and once the fishes enter the trap, they seem to seek an exit at the periphery rather than through the middle. You can leave the traps baited or unbaited but, if you are interested in the larger fishes, do use bait.

If you want the smaller aquarium-size fishes, you'll have to use a type of hardware cloth around the trap; typical chickenwire or mesh is too large for the capture of tiny species. Incidentally, don't discount the possibility of approaching trap fishermen and offering to take the smaller varieties that are of no interest to them. Many collectors have worked out an agreement with trap fishermen—the collector services the traps, and in return has his choice of the day's catch.

Once you've caught your fish, be gentle with it. It's important to handle specimens as little as possible. A fish is covered, on its outer surface, not with hard scales but with a fragile epidermis and mucus that protects it against fungi and other death-dealing parasites. If this outer layer is removed, as it inevitably is in part by nets and handling, the areas of removal, roughly equivalent to "burns," become avenues of invasion for infection.

A badly "burned" fish has little chance for survival. Your best bet is to transfer the fish, while still in the water, from the net, bottle, slurp-gun, or other capturing device into a water-filled container. This water should be freshly taken from the sea or lake where the specimen was living. Even Sea Anemones, many varieties of which are ideal for home aquar-

Good balance and a highly discriminating eye can make all the difference between success and failure in fish collection.

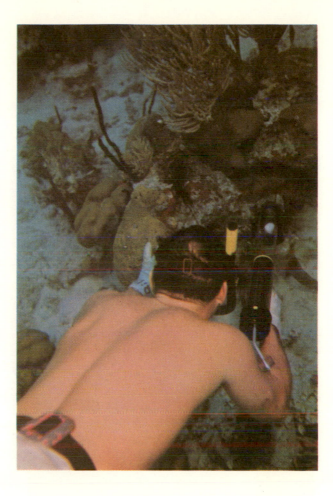

When you have located your specimen, allow the fish to investigate your slurp-gun. It might swim right into the barrel!

iums, must be peeled gently from smooth rocks; if the membrane that adheres to the rock is torn, the anemone will invariably die.

You must decide whether you intend to keep the specimens for yourself, or, as many are doing, collect for profit. Unquestionably, there is money to be made in selling the various brilliantly colored fishes. In many areas spearfishermen are trading their harpoons for slurp-guns and collecting-cages. Added to the obvious profit involved is the great sport of trapping the elusive underwater creatures. In the light of the more than 250,000 marine aquariums in the United States, ranging in size from two and a half to fifty gallons, it's little wonder that the demand for aquarium fishes is so great.

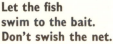

Let the fish
swim to the bait.
Don't swish the net.

When transporting fishes, *always* fill whatever container used with the same water in which the fish was caught. This is a must. The size of the container is the next consideration: a 16″ × 16″ fish-shipping box will safely accommodate a dozen 1½″-long salt-water fishes, or about 15 of the fresh-water varieties. A good rule to follow is not to exceed more than four fishes to 100 square inches of water surface.

Most of your collecting will be done in sunny weather, and it is important that the container water does not become overheated. The higher the water temperature, the less oxygen can be dissolved in it. Higher temperature drives oxygen out of solution. Many a day's work has been for nought because the collector left the fish-filled containers exposed to the hot sun.

With cotton gloves the collector can readily handle most specimens of marine life. A small Hawksbill Turtle was this day's catch.

Use plastic bags that fit loosely into the container. Fill the plastic bags, inside the container, with four inches of water; then allow about five minutes of compressed oxygen to bubble through the water. (Oxygen, in most cases, can be obtained from a surgical-supply house, or even from a welding shop.) If you are transporting the fishes by automobile, you might use styrofoam pails as safety containers. Sufficient oxygen, for short trips, will enter the water as it sloshes around the container.

If the fishes are to be shipped by air freight, first squeeze all air out of the plastic bags; then refill the bags with oxygen, tie the top of the bags and place them in the protective cartons for shipping. The fishes will then be swimming in water over which an atmosphere of oxygen drifts and which will freely

109

A snorkeler "sweeps" the underwater playground for marine specimens for her aquarium.

enter the water. A pack set up like this should keep the fishes alive for about twenty-four hours—ample time to reach their destination.

Keeping salt-water fishes in an environment different from their natural habitat is no longer the chore it was a few years ago. Of course, they are not generally adaptable to basic changes, but with proper equipment and care, they can easily be maintained in your home aquarium.

Contrary to general opinion, the success of a salt-water aquarium is not dependent upon a source of pure sea water. It becomes a simple matter to obtain water for the marine aquarium by using artificial sea-water preparations that are now available.

There should be no metal of any kind in contact with the water. Unlike fresh water, salt water is destructive of metals and the slightest trace of dissolved metals in the water could be enough to poison the fishes. Lead has been used in some instances, but there's always the possibility that it might contain some impurities which could be toxic to the fishes. Even the

This Yellow-tail Demoiselle on Star Coral is in its iridescent jewel phase.

use of lead decorations manufactured for use in fresh-water aquariums is inadvisable for your salt-water aquarium. Keep the water level in the tank below the metal rim. If the rim and metal edges haven't been painted with black asphaltum varnish, do so before placing your specimens inside.

Keep the aquarium covered with a glass top to insure that evaporation is kept to a minimum. Your aquarium should be fitted with an artificial aerator which facilitates proper gas exchange—providing sufficient oxygen and eliminating carbon dioxide and other wastes.

Try to keep your aquarium temperature at about 72° F. but this can vary for most species. Keep the tank shielded from direct rays of the sun; if, however, the tank does become too warm, remove the cover for a short period until the water has cooled sufficiently.

The colors of most marine animals, except those of mollusc shells, are likely to change with preservation. Perfect results depend upon experience.

Basically, there are two types of specimens you will be

The precious Red Coral of southern France is a "treasure" for adventurous collectors.

concerned with preserving: dry, such as Starfish, Sea Urchins, Sponges, Coral, etc.; and liquid, such as Sea Anemones, plant life, and soft-bodied animals, which must be preserved in liquid.

Dry specimens are the easiest to prepare for preservation, but they must first be *thoroughly* dried. A low-temperature oven or an infra-red lamp will aid this process, or you can even air-dry them in the shade. Remember not to store or mount partially dried specimens in air-tight containers. Many of the specimens will retain unpleasant odors after drying, but this can be prevented by soaking the animal in 70 per cent alcohol (rubbing alcohol will do) or 10 per cent formalin for twenty-four hours before drying. Be sure to rinse the specimen in fresh water and dry thoroughly.

If there is any possibility that your specimen might be attacked by insects, soak the creature in a saturated borax solution before drying.

The animals should be doped so that their muscles will not

contract on fixation. This is especially important for delicate animals, and for sea-snails which are likely to contract back into their shells. It is less important for large, solid animals with internal or external skeletons. Fishes are best killed by dropping them into 70 per cent ethanol alcohol, and then fixing in formalin, though fresh water is a more convenient narcotic for marine invertebrates. Keep them in the water for several hours at least.

Except when anæsthetizing with fresh water, ideally each animal should be set aside in a separate container of water, big enough for it to extend in and away from light and disturbance until it is fully relaxed. Then add the narcotic gently.

If the animal is fixed before it is fully narcotized, it will

Indiscriminate use of fish traps often depletes off-shore marine life of its most colorful species, and the markers for the traps present a constant boating hazard.

contract. If it is left too long, it will die and begin to digest itself away, spoiling the fine structure while the animal still seems perfectly fresh. Test for narcosis by poking with a pin, and fix when the animal fails to respond. Don't prod too often, or the animal may pass out while partly contracted. It will take several hours for full narcosis.

Pour off the narcotic solution, replace by fixative, and leave to stand for several hours at the least.

Perhaps the best general fixative for marine animals is neutral formaldehyde solution. Take care that no animals having calcareous plates are treated with formaldehyde, however, as the formaldehyde may eat away the calcium structure of the shells. When using neutral formaldehyde, add a little calcium carbonate (limestone or natural chalk) to the solution, both in the storage bottle you are using and in each container with specimens. As long as the carbonate is visible, the solution is safe.

Ten per cent formalin is the best general preservative. Use one part of commercial formaldehyde (available at most

Small fishes can be attracted for collection (or photographing) by chopping up some of the Sea Urchins you find along the bottom.

Starfish are often found in shallow off-shore waters that are accessible to the snorkeler.

drugstores) to 9 parts of water. There is sometimes confusion between formaldehyde and formalin. Formaldehyde is a gas which dissolves in water to form a saturated solution of 40 per cent by weight. This saturated solution is formalin. Weak solutions won't preserve tissues but will cause them to break up or soften. It is very important not to use weak solutions with very watery animals whose body fluids greatly dilute the preservative. For very small, soft-bodied animals, a 5 per cent formalin solution is good. Add one part formaldehyde to 19 parts water.

When labelling, it's a good idea to note what fixative and preservative you've used. The information on the label can be as important as the specimen itself. Without, at the very least, an identifiable locality of collection, many specimens would more likely go down the drain than under a microscope.

Labels stuck or tied to the specimen container are very likely to be lost or defaced, and numbered tags and notebook entries to be separated. It is best to put the basic information into the preservative with the specimen, but it takes a tough paper to stand this for long. A good goatskin parchment paper is ideal. Use India ink when completing permanent labels; if a pencil is used for the temporary label, be sure to use a soft lead. Paper is more resistant when none of the fibres have been broken, so use a rather broad smooth point.

An excellent idea is to make your label while underwater, noting the things that you might forget after returning to shore. Plastic slates are available for this purpose, and a simple lead pencil on a string attached to the slate can accompany you on each dive. The following data should be taken on your slate: *Locality; Depth; Date; Habitat* (rocks, crevice, found on bottom,

The Sea-Cucumber (to which the snorkeler is pointing with his knife) is commonly found on the sandy bottom near coral heads. The Japanese eat these creatures.

An intrepid diver brings a huge, encrusted Conch Shell up from its reef confines.

etc.); *Frequency* (how many seen, common, rare, etc.); *Associations* (with own species, in pairs, solitary, parasite, host, etc.); *Water conditions* (temperature, turbulence, abundance of plankton, etc.).

Lobsters and other large crustaceans intended for mounting should be fixed for several days in 10 per cent formalin solution and then dried. Arrange the legs in approximately the desired positions prior to soaking in the formalin solution, as the joints become stiffened and difficult to manipulate. Minor adjustments can be made when the specimen is set up to dry. While drying, the appendages should be held in place by pins, tacks and whatever supports seem necessary. After the specimen is thoroughly dry, coat it with transparent liquid plastic and allow to cure until completely hardened. Color is preserved moderately well

117

The Coquille St.
Jacques, or Giant
Scallop, is brought up
from the chilly French
waters.

A gourmet's delight is
the Scallop. This one
was captured near the
English Channel.

after formalin fixation and drying, but will fade quickly in strong light. For the starfishes, relax them in warm water, then place in the same solution of 10 per cent formalin. Allow the specimens to harden for about twenty-four hours in the formalin and then thoroughly dry in a "warm" oven or in the shade.

Gathering shells is an age-old pastime. No other specimens are as widely collected, bought, and sold for their rarity and beauty. Unusual shapes, interesting histories and practical uses have combined to make the collecting and study of seashells (conchology) one of the foremost hobbies in the world.

As a snorkeler, you have a distinct advantage over the less adventurous collectors because the most perfect specimens are found living on the ocean floor, only a dive away. Search everywhere, in rock and coral crevices, along sandy stretches and off the rocky shoreline.

Many of the shells found will be empty, but if the animal is present, remove it by placing the shell in moderately hot water for a few minutes. Hang the shell up over a soft landing place with a small hook attached to the animal to aid in separating him from the shell. This same technique can be used to remove conchs from their beautiful shells as well. Label your shells much as you did other marine specimens you've collected. Incidentally, most shell collectors prefer their specimens in their natural state, but if you want some of the shells as decorative pieces, the epidermis can be removed easily by soaking the shell in a solution of caustic soda. Add one pound to a gallon of water.

The Giant Scallop, or Coquille St. Jacques, is a well known "edible scallop" off French shores. One of the most interesting feats to witness is this large shellfish swimming rapidly after fish! The Scallop moves swiftly through the water by opening and closing the valves of its shell. Kept in pens in some French coastal areas, they can be easily observed.

Massive boulders of living coral grow as each generation of polyps adds a tiny layer to the deposits of its ancestors. Some resemble flowers, such as the Flower Coral seen in the lower middle of this photo.

MARINE LIFE –
CORALS AND SPONGES

The reef has been called the world's most extensive hunting ground for the coral fancier, shell collector, underwater explorer and photographer. Truly, it is a fairyland of colors, and the colors fluctuate from hour to hour depending on whether the tentacles of the coral are exposed or withdrawn. So scarcely perceptible are these hues that an exquisite array of soft color at close range seems a drab wasteland a few feet away.

Countless millions of limestone-depositing sea organisms first began a reef's unending creation. Coral, the aggregation of limy skeletons of untold numbers of tiny sea animals takes a multitude of forms. Formations grow upward as each new generation adds a tiny layer to the deposits of past ages. Though coral lives in all seas, even as far north as Norway's fjords, the reef-building varieties thrive only in tropical and subtropical shallows.

Some corals bear a striking resemblance to lettuce—some resemble the convolutions of the brain, the underside of a

Named for its resemblance to antlers, the Elkhorn Coral seems to be spreading its arms in welcome to fishes and snorkelers alike. Note the camouflaged Trunkfishes gliding between the antlers.

mushroom, the pipes of an organ, or a dainty gathering of lace. Others compare to large pillars, forests of bristling staghorns or elkhorns, and still more take on a likeness to stars, fingers, and flowers.

The minute coral animals, long mistaken for plants, are true cousins of Jellyfish; but unlike the Jellyfish, the primitive corals are free-swimming only as embryos. Early in life the tube-like polyps imprison themselves in limestone dungeons, secreted, as a rule, on their ancestors' skeletons. By day most corals shrink into their stone castles; at night they extend tentacles to catch plankton and carry it to their mouths.

A major requirement of the reef corals is that the temperature of the surrounding sea water does not drop more than a few degrees below 20° C. or 70° F. for more than a short time. Prolonged exposure to slightly lower temperatures or shorter exposure to much reduced temperatures both result in the death of the reef corals.

It is true that the delicate branching coral of the Norwegian

This huge ball of coral has the convolutions of the human brain, and is not unnaturally called Brain Coral.

fjords has been dredged from a depth of over 1,000 feet, but true reef corals are always found in fairly shallow depths near warm shores. Usually these are in less than 150 feet of water, with the most active growth taking place within 90 feet of the surface. This rate of growth increases with the temperature of the water and varies with the different species. The ramified, or branching kinds, spread much more rapidly than the compact, spherical shapes. It is also believed that coral has a maximal size. Once this is reached, all growth ceases. As the coral polyps need a great deal of oxygen for their reef building, they are best nourished and develop best towards the open sea where the waves constantly bring new supplies of water rich in plankton and oxygen.

The Pillar Coral (*Dendrogyra cylindrus*) looks very much like a deformed human hand. The small compact stone towers it builds are so solid that they will survive life in shallow waters where most of the branching kinds are broken off by the force of the beating waves. Look for colonies of the heavy, branching, columnar cylinders which rise vertically from the

Staghorn Coral differs from Elkhorn both in size and in being more pointed. Examine a tip closely, and you might find it is a live polyp. A Painted Parrotfish swims in front.

Beware of the Fire Coral with its vertical plates! Rubbing against this stinging coral is not dangerous but it is painful. Use gloves in handling.

bottom on all reefs, especially in open back-reef waters. Pillar coral may attain a height of three feet.

You might be surprised to know that the Fire or Stinging Coral (*Millepora complanata*) that is so common to warm waters is not a true coral at all, though it is very similar. The Fire Coral group does not produce chalk-secreting forms. Colonies form vertical flattened plates which generally grow facing the direction of wave travel. The Fire Corals grow into small branches and often form encrustations on the surface of old coral or dead Sea Fans. Its bright mustard-yellow color makes this false coral easily recognizable and, therefore, easy to

Timid reef dwellers dart coyly among the stumps of Pillar Coral.

avoid. Wear your gloves! Although the stinging cells of the Fire Coral are painful, it is not dangerous and the pain is not long-lasting.

The delicate Staghorn Coral (*Acropora cervicornis*) is particularly fragile. It forms veritable hedges six or seven feet high, and thanks to its long branches, it is well protected against being covered by sand. However, in very violent storms the whole reef is sometimes buried in drift sand, and dies off. You will usually find Staghorn Coral on the inside of lagoons. On the

125

Common in southern Atlantic waters is the Star Coral. Each little group of polyps, as it calcifies, forms a shape resembling a star.

windward side of reefs, it can occur at depths greater than ten feet.

One of the most commonly seen corals is the Elkhorn Coral (*Acropora palmata*). Colonies of this coral form flattened, branching plates of variable extent. The branches extend outward from a short, thick trunk. In the back reefs, small finger-like branches form at the edge of the flattened plates.

Another very common coral you will see is the Star Coral (*Montastrea*). Some of these colonies form boulders which may attain a great size (up to five feet across). There are many related colonies which also have the star-like polyps, so don't be too quick to identify this coral too precisely.

The Brain Corals, too, have a great many related groups. Some are quite large and are almost perfectly symmetrical, but can be most easily identified as some type of Brain Coral by the telltale valleys (convolutions) that greatly resemble the human brain. In one group of Brain Corals (*Diploria clivosa*) the convolutions are sinuous near the middle but lose their sinuosity towards the edge of the colony.

Later, as you begin collecting, you may find some of your best specimens secreted beneath huge boulders of Brain Coral. (Incidentally, the little clinging fishes that you often see swarming through the Brain Coral's narrow valleys are Gobies.)

The soft corals do not form any cohesive skeletal structure, but are composed of microscopically small chalk-like needles which afford protection against fishes which feed on coral. These soft coral grow chiefly in the more placid waters and are found throughout the reef's shallows. You will find them slimy to the touch, leathery of texture, dark in color, and often of great size. Sea Fans, Sea Whips, Bush Gorgonians, and Sea Plumes are composed primarily of a horny material called gorgonin which allows these non-stony corals to form dense beds in areas where wave action would break stiff stony coral.

This Brain Coral boasts a lovely flock of Feather Duster Worms. Swimming calmly by is a Squirrel Fish.

Waving to and fro in the current is a Gorgonian Sea Fan, serving as a backdrop for a small Wrasse.

The Sea Fans add a great amount of lime to the resilient skeleton. Though having less flexibility than some of the other non-stony corals, they often grow attached to corals in calmer waters. The precious Red Coral of the Mediterranean, which you will find later when you begin collecting, is also a member of this group. The Red Coral's skeleton, however, is composed almost entirely of bright red lime. Although the Gorgonians are not primary reef builders, like their stony-coral cousins, they are largely tropical in distribution.

A good deal of scientific study is taking place at present, because even today it is not known exactly why the reef-forming corals only flourish down to depths of 150 feet. There are individual deeper growths, such as the Red Coral of the Mediterranean and the orange-colored, fleshy Flower Coral of Norway, but these do not form reefs. It is possible that the polyps are dependent on the supplementary source of oxygen that is received from algae which live within the polyp's tissue. As with all plants, algae must take in oxygen and give off carbon dioxide—and must have sunlight. The sun does not penetrate

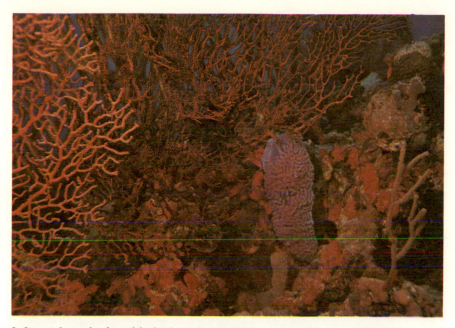

Soft coral can be found in its lacy form swaying gently as you snorkel by. The lovely lavender creature in the foreground is an Azure Sponge.

much deeper than 150 feet into the sea, so it is quite probable that it is the algae itself which determines the limited depth to which reef corals are able to grow.

These, then, are the reef builders: the stony corals and the soft corals, the stinging coral, and even the hard coralline algae that splash upon the rocklike lavender cement. Working together, their complex interplay gives rise to the enormous bulk of the reef. And so the reef grows, an intricate community of many colorful forms of life.

Of all the animals on the reef, sponges are perhaps the most primitive.

Sponges constitute a principal division of the animal kingdom. Because of their plant-like qualities, however, they were not recognized as true animals until the nineteenth century. The phylum name, Porifera, or "pore-bearer," is derived from the image of a sponge as a vase perforated by holes.

Distribution of sponges is world-wide and at all depths of water. A few species live in the intertidal zone, where twice daily they are exposed to the atmosphere. The vast majority,

The surfaces of sponges vary. The brown Tubular Sponge seen here is soft and pliable, but its surface is spur-like. Other sponges are hard and brittle. The Golden Vase Sponge in the foreground has a cheese-like texture.

Soft Tube Sponges nestle among soft Gorgonian Sea Whips.

however, can exist only below the surface in the salinity of ocean water.

Knowledge of sponge nutrition is somewhat limited. However, they obviously extract planktonic food from the water circulated through the vase by the beating of the flagella, the long lash-like appendage serving as an organ of locomotion of cells.

Accurate identification of sponges, as with many of the corals, is often difficult because of the wide range of common characteristics. The color red, for example, is typical of many different varieties, and a few species even have alternate colors.

Sponges exist in varied sizes and shapes: the largest are enormous, sometimes larger than a small barrel; and the most contrasting forms, tubular and spherical, live in warm, shallow waters. Perhaps the outstanding feature of sponges is their colors. They occur in every hue imaginable, with each species having a characteristic shade that changes with its environment. Sponges growing in good lighting have darker and more vivid colors, while those living in regions with less light are dull and more drab in appearance. The brilliant blue-purple Azure

Vase is perhaps one of the loveliest of the sponges, and relatively common, too.

Certain encrusting sponges, in yellow, lavender, purple, or red, are frequently found on the surface of coral, wrecks, and native fish-pots. A few branching sponges actually grow on the sea floor.

An interesting feature of sponges is their power to regenerate: if broken into pieces, each fragment is capable of forming a new sponge. In addition, both asexual and sexual reproduction occur in sponges.

A few examples of symbiotic relationships exist between

A diver studies gnarled formations of coral and sponge growing rampant on the framework of a lost fish trap.

certain species of sponges and several species of crabs. Sponge grows on the shell occupied by a Hermit Crab and eventually covers and dissolves it, forming a new home for the crab. This is a case where the crab doesn't eat the sponge—it wears it! This is a form of mutualism: the sponge benefits by transportation, while the Hermit Crab is protected from predators. Sponge doesn't taste too good, but crabs do!

As a snorkeler you may find enormous sponges such as the Basket Sponge above, which is larger than a small barrel. The conical Basket Sponge below is surrounded by growths of coral and soft Red Sponge.

Red is typical of many varieties of sponge, but for reasons still unknown a few species such as those in the foreground here have two alternate colors. In the background are a clump of Fire Coral and branches of Staghorn Coral.

In regard to relationships, 17,000 small animals were collected from a single giant Atlantic specimen. A familiar U.S. East Coast sponge is the Dead Men's Fingers. Its bleached skeleton is often found washed ashore. The common household sponge comes from the Mediterranean. The dried and treated skeletons of a few species also come from the southern Atlantic. The commercial sponge industry, today, has been affected by such synthetic materials as plastics from which many of our bath sponges are now made.

One of the most beautiful sponges of tropical waters is the red-fringed Basket Sponge found off Jamaica. Many of the flexible Tube Sponges will also be seen as you wend your way along the reef.

Sea Anemones are frequently associated with corals and the limestone "castles" are often encrusted with the anemone's brightly colored growths. Minute stinging darts lining the Sea Anemone's tentacles paralyze most small creatures touching them, but some small fishes—for reasons no one knows—live intimately with the anemone, even diving unscathed into its bed of tentacles.

Anemones vary in size from a tiny $\frac{1}{4}$ inch to the giant three-foot-wide Stoicactis of the Great Barrier Reef of Australia. Most anemones are quite difficult to spot as they prefer to hide in crevices with only their tentacles exposed, awaiting their prey.

Like the corals and sponges, Sea Anemones are living animals; unlike the coral polyps, however, the Anemones do not secrete limestone. Although much bigger than the coral animal, their basic structure is the same—a hollow tube with a mouth and tentacles at one end. Their tentacles are quite thick and fleshy, and you will be able to see that they are almost like the petals of a flower.

Though Sea Anemones are abundant on the coral reef, they are also found in many other parts of the world. And like the other reef dwellers, they take on a variety of forms. Small Anemones are often brilliantly decorated, as are many of the smaller inhabitants of the underwater world. The bigger

Sea Anemones are animals that look like plants. They are frequently associated with corals, and rocks are often encrusted with their brightly colored growths. Here, an Anemone has developed in the midst of Star Coral beds. With lightning speed its waving arms will close over any small fish that comes within its deadly range.

Marine worms are segmented, with each part bearing bristles. In several species the spines are detachable and can prick the skin if touched, causing a sting. Pictured above and below are two types of Feather Duster Worms.

anemones, on the other hand, are usually drab in appearance. These larger anemones are able to feed on small fish, shrimp, and certain crabs.

The Hermit Crab, it seems, has worked out several convenient arrangements with his marine fellows. Just as the crab spends a great deal of his time "wearing" the latest in sponges, he also allows small stinging anemones to attach themselves to his shell. You might see as many as seven or eight anemones riding the same shell—few creatures can boast of such dedicated protection! And don't think for a moment that the big Hermit Crab does not appreciate this service, for when he moves to a larger-shelled home, he takes his anemones with him. He carefully detaches the anemones with his claws and transfers them to the new shell.

As an avid underwater explorer, you will find the Sea Anemones' brilliant hues of red, green, and white one of the reef's most enticing sights.

As the sponges added to the growing reef—so, in turn, do the Tube Worms and Anemones. Many of the Sea Worms, often called Feather Dusters, will be found burrowed into the living coral home for protection. They are lined with a hard porcelain-like material, and, when undisturbed, the head of the living worm looks like a beautifully colored flower. A slight movement or shadow will cause retraction into the burrow, often so quickly that the movement is undetectable.

Waving lazily like peacock fans, the handsome, delicate, feathery structures flutter in the water beyond the edge of the tube, bringing oxygen and food to the hidden worm. Those who do not bore into the living coral, fashion tubes of sand or shells glued together with mucus, and live attached to the coral without actually harming it.

Many questions enter your mind while swimming along the aged grating of a wreck. Where was the ship bound? Who was aboard? Why did it sink?

TREASURE DIVING

We have all heard yarns about sunken shipwrecks laden with undiscovered treasure; these tales frequently crop up in the diver's world. Sometimes the stories are just figments of overactive imaginations—mere wishful thinking. But there is one definite reality; treasure valued at many millions has been, and is right now being, reclaimed from Atlantic and Caribbean waters. One of the most recent finds was in the shallows off Florida's east coast, well within the range of snorkel divers. Where does this treasure come from?

From the 15th to the 18th centuries, a flotilla of Spanish galleons gathered yearly in Havana, Cuba. Gold, silver, and jewels filled the holds—loot collected from the annual intake of wealth from all Spanish America, at that time part of colonial Spain. From the Havana rendezvous, the ships rode the Gulf Stream up the Straits of Florida to cross the Atlantic for Spain.

On July 31, 1715, one such fleet found itself near a rocky shore (now Cape Kennedy) when a furious hurricane struck. Winds and waves smashed the fleet on to the cape. Only one ship escaped destruction, and more than a thousand lives and treasure worth millions were lost.

Alongside the sponge-encrusted ship's hull comes a steady stream of visitors—three large Snappers, a striped Sergeant-Major, a female Yellowhead Wrasse, a Blue (black) Tang, and a school of tiny Silversides. (The water is unnaturally deep blue because the picture was shot from a darkened area inside the wreck.)

It is said that survivors camped on shore and tried to recover what they could of the sunken treasure; about a quarter of it was retrieved. However, pirates attacked and looted the camp, ending the salvage attempt.

Currently, a company of intrepid divers, adventurers all, are recovering doubloons, pieces-of-eight, and priceless jewels from the Florida shallows.

When lightships and lighthouses, radio telephony, and efficient means of communication were only beginning, the sea still took many vessels and many lives. There were various reasons why these ships went down. Some were caught in storms and forced to surrender before the violence of nature; many were destroyed during naval engagements; errors in navigation were responsible for others; and still more were slowly demolished by worms, electrolysis, and rot.

Today, modern vessels ply the shipping lanes with precision and safety. Regulations control the manner in which the safety of cargo passengers is insured. The chances of a vessel becoming lost at sea or running afoul of rocks or shore are minimized to a degree where it is almost impossible to lose a ship. Such care is taken with communications from ship to ship and from ship to shore by various means that a distressed vessel can be assisted in a matter of hours, sometimes minutes.

For centuries man has been building ships and going to sea, and most of his crafts have long since settled to the bottom. It might seem that the sea floor is literally covered with wreckage, and the task of finding a sunken ship simple. But the destructive forces of nature that are ever working against man's handiwork on land are also present under the sea. Sunken ships fall apart very rapidly. However, one thing is now certain—there *is* treasure to be found, and divers, true-life adventurers, are finding it.

Knowing where to look, what to look for, and even when to look are fundamentals. There are hundreds of sunken ships laden with treasure that has never been discovered. Finding and exploring a wreck in the shallows of the ocean's floor is

Discovering and exploring a wreck in the shallows of the ocean's floor is a unique and thrilling experience, and one you must not miss.

When diving on a wreck there is always the hope of finding treasure. Perhaps something valuable is hidden here.

Even a number or symbol on this massive propeller could provide a key to the mystery.

A curious barracuda appears somewhat annoyed by your unexpected intrusion into his domain.

a fascinating experience, but with nothing as a guide, you could spend endless time searching in vain.

Divers are forever seeking new information that may lead to the discovery of wreck sites. A superficial search will sometimes reveal locations, but the best areas and data will be found through extensive research, examining microfilm of old newspapers, Navy records, files of marine insurance companies, and the publications and archives of historical societies and museums.

In tropical and sub-tropical waters you will have to have a sharp eye to find a wreck, for the layers of limestone are sometimes many inches thick where coral has been growing. Anchors, occasionally lost by ships when caught in rocks and reefs, may indicate the presence of a wreck nearby. If you find no valuables on the surface of a wreck, don't be deceived into thinking that nothing of value remains on the ship. Often, the most valuable objects are found underneath.

After being in salt water for many years, silver takes on a black crust of silver sulphide if it is not touching iron—electrolysis does not take place when these metals are in contact. Gold, when found in sand or mud is usually bright and clean, if it has not been affected by salt water. Copper and brass objects just beneath the surface take on a light-green tinge when covered with coral limestone. If wood has been buried in the sand or covered with tar, it should survive the ravages of teredo worms.

Scan the bottom carefully for anything that looks odd. Remember, the only clue to a lost galleon could be a pile of ballast stones, or a cannon covered with coral!

While swimming among the coral- and sponge-encrusted remains of a ship, let your curiosity and imagination run free. Where was the ship bound? Who was aboard? Why did it sink? And, hopefully, is there treasure? Each ship has a background as complex as the human beings aboard her. What causes a shipwreck? What act long before singles out the members of the crew who are to die? And who to live? Sometimes, through research, these questions can be answered; often they cannot be. In the wreck you are exploring in the accompanying photographs, most of these mysteries have been solved.

The *Rhone*, a new and fine addition to the Royal Mail fleet, sank off the British Virgin Island of Salt on October 29, 1867. The Royal Mail liner was making her maiden voyage from England to the West Indies and was at anchor near Peter Island, one of the chain of islands bounding Sir Francis Drake Channel to the south and east of Tortola. The *Rhone* was only four weeks out of Southampton and preparing for the return crossing.

At about 11 o'clock on the morning of the 29th, the barometer suddenly began to fall, the sky darkened, and with a great roar, a savage hurricane fell upon the *Rhone*. As she sought protection in Peter Island's Great Harbor, the wind changed to the north. With engines going at full speed, the ship rode the storm, but a fearful blast struck the *Rhone*, forcing her to attempt an escape, or be trapped against a lee shore.

The "steam-sailer" tried vainly to reach open sea through Salt Island passage, but her engines were no match for the hurricane winds. She struck the rocks off Salt Island where she broke her back, parted amidships and slid into the sea, taking most of her company with her. The men in the stokeholds and all others who were below deck had no chance whatever, and

Small fishes accompany the adventurous wreck diver as he fins through a crusted arch.

must have been killed instantly as the vessel broke up. Of the passengers on board, only one, an Italian, survived. Of the officers and crew, only 21 escaped. The lone passenger-survivor spent the next six hours in the water before he was cast on to a small island where some of the crew had also managed to reach shore.

Thus, the *Rhone* came to her fateful end, taking 135 souls with her. Many of their graves can be found today on a bluff overlooking the wreckage.

Wrecks of any kind usually abound with fish and become unofficial sanctuaries for all forms of marine life. Once the remains of the wreckage are covered with algae and sponge, it becomes a feeding place and shelter for small animals and other crustaceans which in turn attract the larger fishes. Knowing this, fish-watchers, underwater archaeologists, photographers, and spearfishermen haunt these sunken ships, particularly in northern waters where there are no natural reefs.

Wrecks provide large fishes with a place to hide, not so much from larger predators but from wave activity. For the

What secrets lie beneath this corrosion-locked porthole?

groupers and snappers that so frequently inhabit sunken remains, there must be large, and preferably deeply penetrating, passageways in which to retreat. Other fish, such as rays, hake, haddock, and flounders can find protection in their adaptive coloration and by pressing flat against the bottom, and so need not seek the underwater structure of a shipwreck. Often, wrecks provide an even better habitat than some natural reefs of the subtropics.

In California waters you will discover many Rockfish, Kelpfish,

You could easily overlook this large Rock Hind that lies camouflaged among the radiant formations of sponge.

Wrecked ships become unofficial sanctuaries for fishes and other marine life. A Rock Beauty and Spanish Hogfish scurry along a brightly flushed beam.

Wearing a coat of sponge, an ancient Greek water jug (amphora) lies hidden in the deep.

The free-diver, on reaching the amphora, finds it wedged snugly between rocks.

With only mask, snorkel and fins, a free-diver can locate buried treasure in the shallows of the Mediterranean. After finding this 2,000-year-old amphora spout, she struggles to loosen it enough to bring it to the surface intact.

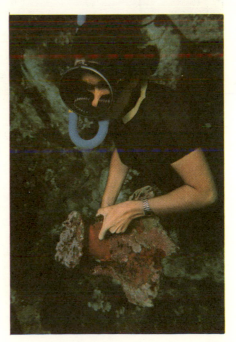

Success at last! The museum piece is hoisted on to the rocky Spanish shore.

and Sandbass as you work your way through the forests of kelp down to an aging hull. Pelagic Yellow-tail and Bonito will be encountered swimming freely around the outer reaches of these wrecks.

After a few dives off the Mediterranean coasts of Spain, Italy, Sicily and Greece, many divers suffer from "amphora fever." There are many traces of ancient wrecks along these coasts which have not yet been fully explored, and amphoræ (the two-handled, narrow-necked vessels used by the ancient Greeks and Romans for holding wine and oil, etc.) are regularly found. Bays which once served as anchorages for Roman and Greek ships, often yield great caches of the age-old pottery. Even shards of Cretan and Carthaginian amphoræ have been uncovered from depths of only 15 feet of water, close to the shore.

When a complete amphora is found, it must be brought clear of rocks or obstacles. Broken fragments partially buried in the sand are a more and more common sight in areas frequented by underwater tourists. These pieces can be of great importance, for they may show a neck design which has not yet been catalogued.

A complete amphora is quite heavy, so lifting-bags will have to be used to raise it to the surface. Probably the most readily available lifting device is a simple beach ball inside a string bag. Take an air-tank below and, after securely attaching the amphora, fill the ball and follow your treasure to the surface. Having a row boat standing by will help to trap the amphora as it breaks the surface, and will make the trip to shore much easier for you—the treasure diver!

UNDERWATER PHOTOGRAPHY

"The tongue cannot utter nor the pen describe all the wonders of the sea."—*Christopher Columbus*. How true!

After exploring and collecting tirelessly, you have now reached a phase in underwater swimming where documenting the splendor of these gardens below the sea becomes very important. Here, the snorkeler becomes a photographer!

Records of underwater photographs date as far back as 1856 when a camera, housed in a not so "waterproof" box was lowered from a small boat to the sea bed three fathoms below. Though the camera did get wet, the photographer did not—he operated the shutter from the boat by means of an 18-foot cord!

A more serious attempt at underwater photography was made by a French photographer who was able to obtain several relatively good photos of sunken ships. Submerged in a water-tight diving bell, he used electric lights to supplement the natural lighting and shot the pictures through a porthole. Much to his credit, he descended to depths of nearly 300 feet where he remained for about ten minutes.

In 1895, Dr. Louis Boutan, another Frenchman, took the

Squid are often willing subjects for the shallow-water photographer. The approach in photography can be likened to the stalking techniques employed by the spearfisherman—silently move in close, and make your shot.

first underwater flash photographs. The "flashgun," consisting of a lighted spirit lamp under a watertight glass dome, was fitted to the top of a large wooden barrel filled with air and oxygen. The flash amounted to only a short burst of light, but he managed to obtain some remarkable photographs.

Perhaps the next significant achievement in the evolution of underwater picture-taking came in 1913 when an American named Williamson filmed the first commercial underwater cinema film. His underwater scenes were used in the film of Jules Verne's "Twenty Thousand Leagues Under the Sea." Like his early predecessors, Williamson worked "dry" by means of a large pressure-resistant sphere equipped with powerful underwater lights.

After this, underwater photography began to grow. Advances in underwater filming became known throughout the world through the thrilling exploits of Cousteau and Hass. Shooting with a camera instead of a spear, they "exposed" the underwater world.

Framing your quarry at the correct distance and angle is a skill that develops with experience. Try for a low shooting angle, as it will give emphasis to the subject. This picture was taken with frontal lighting from flash. In some ways underwater photography is similar to spearfishing because in both there is a "right time" to trigger the release.

Plant and animal plankton are an essential part of the food cycle in the sea but, to the underwater photographer, these free-swimming microscopic animals are a nuisance. Like other suspended particles, clouds of plankton greatly reduce underwater visibility and play havoc with most underwater filming—particularly if lights are being used, as the particles reflect light back through the lens, causing spots to appear on the exposed film.

Seasonal variations in the density of plankton result in changes in visibility. Plankton cannot tolerate very strong light, so shallow waters are clearest in the summer when the light is strongest. In deeper water, the transparency varies with the time of the day. In mid-summer, the clarity of the water is greatest near the surface at noontime. The plankton migrate towards the surface as the light fades, leaving the deep water clearer.

Water clarity in and near ports or close to river estuaries will vary considerably with tidal conditions. Clearer water from the sea flows in as the tide rises so, if you intend to photograph in such areas, choose a time of day when high tide corresponds with the best lighting conditions—about midday.

Generally speaking, any camera that takes pictures can be used underwater. This is true, but with one important qualification: the camera must be encased in some type of waterproof housing which will keep it safe and dry, and at the same time allow for easy operation of its controls. The range of available housings made today is extensive. If you have a camera, you can be sure that someone makes an underwater case for it. However, before you invest in a new housing for an old camera, evaluate your underwater camera needs.

To begin with, it is difficult to focus accurately underwater. Remember that both you and your subject may drift with the current, so, ideally, you should have a camera that is compact and easy to handle. Since you will be spending a great deal of time in the water, you certainly won't want to be bothered with changing film after taking eight to twelve exposures. This would involve removing the housing, changing film, and re-fitting the housing. An avid photographer could spend more time above water than below!

You should have a camera that handles a large film load, that is, at least 20 exposures or more, if possible. For maximum ease in handling, a lever that releases the shutter, advances film, and re-cocks the shutter is a must. Interchangeable lenses are valuable if you intend to vary your work. For underwater filming you need a wide-angle lens to begin with. Normal lenses are about 50 mm. focal length for 35 mm. cameras, and 75 mm. for 2¼" cameras. Any lenses of substantially shorter lengths are "wide angle." You should be able to approach as close as possible to most underwater subjects and still include a sufficiently wide angle of view.

In 1964, Nikon perfected a camera which fulfills all these criteria. This camera, the Nikonos, seems to be the logical solution to underwater photography. The camera is watertight in itself, which means no external housing is required. Called "amphibious," the Nikonos works in the air as well as in water. Although the manufacturer rates the camera to a depth of

This is a composition to strive for in your underwater shots: man and fish at the bottom of the reef.

160 feet, we have used it successfully at depths of over 200 feet in the Mediterranean. Several photos included in your *Guide to the Underwater* show the Nikonos in action, and all photographs in the *Guide* were taken with this deceptively simple-looking camera.

The Nikonos was chosen for this project because we needed a camera that was ready to dive when *we* were and would be as functional as our other diving gear. After a day's diving, we simply hose off the Nikonos with fresh water right along with our other equipment. Don't attempt this with any other camera that is not enclosed in a housing!

The body of the Nikonos is specially treated die-cast metal.

All exposed parts are corrosion-resistant and internal parts are anti-corrosion treated.

Optically, the Nikonos comes fitted with a Nikkor 35 mm. f2.5 lens with lens focuses from 2¾ feet to infinity in air. The operative depth of field is automatically shown as the aperture is changed. This camera can also be furnished with a specially designed 28 mm. f3.5 lens which has a crisply sharp resolution underwater. Also available for the Nikonos is an interchangeable 21 mm. lens and an extreme wide-angle "Fish-eye" lens.

Shutter speeds go from 1/30th to 1/500th second, plus B for time exposures. Both electronic flash and flash bulbs are synchronized with the designated shutter speed. Two exterior milled-edge knobs control diaphragm adjustment and focus, giving the diver complete control over each picture. The Nikonos has a distinct advantage over an earlier French model of the same design, as filters and close-up lenses can be threaded directly into the Nikonos' normal lens or lens shade.

Without a doubt, the all-weather Nikonos is truly a diver's camera, as functional as mask, fins, and snorkel.

As a camera enthusiast, be alert to unusual situations. Here is a barracuda near the anchor-line. The spots in the background are reflections of light from plankton on the film.

Films for underwater photography are chosen with the same considerations as for top-side shooting. The visibility of the particular waters where you intend to shoot, however, are a determining factor. Faster films will have to be used in areas of poor visibility, especially where color exposures are desired.

Begin your underwater work with black-and-white film; it is inexpensive and there is more of a chance that you will have better results the first time out than if you choose color film for your initial shooting. Plus X is a good all-round film for

For scenes in shallow reef areas, use a filter with discretion because it could destroy the "underwater atmosphere." This Nurse Shark was taken in natural light without a filter.

most waters; if, however, you are fortunate to begin in crystal-clear, well-illuminated waters, you can use Panatomic X Improved. This film is extremely fine-grained but slower than medium-grained Plus X. If visibility in your area is particularly poor, then black-and-white Tri X is for you. Though more grainy than Panatomic or Plus X, the faster Tri X is often called on for filming in deep waters where the amount of light is greatly reduced. Sharpness and definition suffer somewhat when using fast films, but at times there is no choice. Later, when you add flash to your camera, you will be able to move up to the slower emulsions.

Whichever of the black-and-white films you choose, use it over and over until you are familiar with its particularities. Confusion often results when an underwater photographer experiments with several different films. To be certain you don't forget which type is in the camera, tape the box-flap

Underneath ledges and coral heads are good places for photographing. In these protected areas, marine animals feel secure and are more willing to pose. Bounce flash can often be used to achieve unusual effects.

(giving film name) directly to the body of your camera. Even professionals forget from time to time!

Before beginning with color films for underwater photography, there are several facts you should be aware of. First, because of absorption of sunlight, available light photography is limited to shallow water. The sea water acts as a blue-green filter and removes other colors from the white-light spectrum

When you have a cave set-up, utilize the natural light from outside as side and back lighting, along with flash and a low shooting angle, to give depth to your picture.

of the sun. In effect, this means that color film exposed in depths greater than 30 or 40 feet will appear monochromatic, as only blue, green, and a few modified yellows remain.

Red in the spectrum is quickly absorbed by the water, so most underwater pictures will appear quite greenish or bluish. This effect can be corrected by using filters, such as a Color Compensating Red Filter (CCR), which come in a series of numbers (densities). A CCR filter is to be used in waters that tend towards blue with little green, or a Color Compensating Magenta (CCM) if the water tends towards yellow with a definite green tinge.

For black-and-white film, try the Color Correcting Yellow (CCY) series of filters. This CCY filter improves contrast with black-and-white film by cutting through any watery haze and cancelling out certain colors which destroy the effect of black-and-white photographs. A CC filter will correct poor color balance, but the filter, by itself, cannot restore a color lost through absorption. Remember to increase filter number as depth increases.

Hand-held flash and shooting from above bring out interesting high-lights in this large Basket Sponge.

A steady position is essential in all underwater filming. If you are unlucky enough not to be able to brace yourself on the bottom, use a tripod.

Great advances have been made in the manufacture of color films in the past few years. One of the old stand-bys, Koda-chrome II with an ASA 25 (American Standards Association's film rating, according to its speed or sensitivity to light) is an excellent choice *if* you are diving in exceptionally clear waters with bright sunlight filtering through.

Ektachrome X is another outstanding color film for under-water photography. Its greatest advantages are sharpness, contrast, and wonderful colors, besides providing an ASA of 64 which is more than twice that of Kodachrome II.

If you want prints from your underwater exposures, use Kodacolor X with an ASA of 64. The problem with using this negative film underwater is that generally the prints are returned from the processor in colors that are quite different from the ones you remember. Negative material is processed in such a way as to show the complementary colors, and these are trans-ferred to the paper by way of filters. They usually come out much too blue. If you do use negatives, be sure to state on the film package that it was exposed underwater.

Since you will be using a camera that allows you full control with each picture, for most shooting set the shutter speed on the camera at 1/125 (unless your subject is moving exceptionally fast which calls for a 1/250th or even 1/500th on occasion). Change the aperture (f/stop), and also set the distance. Unless you don't mind repeating errors made from previous dives, it is important to keep a constant record of your settings—*while*

Patience and accurate timing were the ingredients that made this unique fish picture.

you are diving. This can be accomplished easily by attaching a pencil (a grease pencil or soft lead pencil) to a plastic slate. Make the necessary notations as you shoot, then transfer the data to a notebook when you return to shore.

Many beginning photographers seal a light-metre in a water-tight jar and take it with them underwater. This can be effective if you do not go too deep. If you are not fortunate enough to have access to a metre, adjust your camera above the surface

163

to light conditions; then, to shoot underwater, simply open the lens one f/stop for each 10 feet as you descend. A dark bottom may require one or two more lens openings—a light-colored bottom requires closing down the lens. These factors, too, should be noted on your writing slate, to be included in your analysis of the prints or transparencies that are returned from the lab.

Remember, too, that if you are using a light-metre you must put the same filter over the metre to avoid having to calculate filter factors with each reading. Gelatin filters are available which can be taped to your metre.

Exposure settings underwater depend on many factors: weather conditions, angle of the sun, clarity of the water, distance of the subject below the surface, color of subject and background, and filters—and not all of these are constant. Experiment!

Your camera lens "sees" the same field you see, so consider the refraction of light rays through the water, and begin by adjusting the distance setting on your camera to 2/3 of the actual distance from the subject (i.e., if the subject is 9 feet from the camera, set it for 6 feet, etc.).

By studying some of the preferred haunts of different forms of marine life, you will be able to position yourself for many wonderful shots before the "action" begins. Don't be content to simply "take a picture." Strive towards a story-line: if people are involved in the shot, have some sort of action demonstrated in the photograph.

Chumming fishes is an excellent way to stage a picture; you can pose the people in your pictures, but the fish may not be so co-operative. When you have located the setting that pleases you, chop up plenty of Sea Urchins and spread around the area. Try not to shoot into open water: the best backdrops for most pictures are the reef, coral heads, schools of fishes, and wrecks. If you need special effects, vary your angles. Some of the most dramatic underwater shots have been taken towards the surface, using natural lighting. Don't underestimate the value of black and white for unique effects. The gloomy atmosphere of a shipwreck is best depicted in black and white.

The only way you can bring out the true colors of depths below about 30 feet is with artificial lighting. This is accom-

When filming in the deep blue (this is 160 feet below the surface of the Mediterranean), you have to balance yourself through proper breathing and positioning with your aqualung. This photographer is using a Bolex 8 mm. motion picture camera in a homemade housing.

plished by using either a strobe-unit, or flash bulbs, the latter being less expensive initially. As a general rule, use clear flash bulbs for all underwater color photography, except for extreme close-ups. The water will filter out predominant reds that clear bulbs emit, giving good color balance to the picture. Blue bulbs used on close shots will produce a more pleasing effect. Although some photographers use clear bulbs in every situation, they do give off too much red and yellow when used at short distances.

Flash exposures underwater will be more difficult than shooting by available light. As you know from top-side filming, you determine the lens opening (f/stop) when using flash by dividing the bulb guide number (as provided by the manu-facturer on the bulb carton) by the distance from camera to subject. This can be accomplished underwater by doubling the lamp-to-subject distance before applying the bulb guide

The wonders of the deep are more readily captured on film than with speargun. The Sting Ray, as the photographer approaches, takes flight, but is caught in a sequence of pictures as he wings along the sandy bottom.

number. The only difficulty here is that water clarity will rarely be the same on two separate occasions. It is, however, a guide line to follow until you can work out your own guide numbers for the waters you dive in. Trial and error is the best method for determining your accurate guide number. This number, incidentally, varies with the type of film and brand of flash bulbs, so keep your underwater slate handy as well as your notebook.

Have an idea of what you want to photograph, set yourself

As the Sting Ray flees, a second photographer with still camera stops him in mid-flight.

for it, and shoot. Being prepared for a shot is sometimes the most important element in obtaining it. Beginning fish photographers usually end up with terrific tail shots. Knowing exactly when to snap the shutter can only come with several rolls of experience. Keep the subject framed in the sportfinder until you see all you want in your picture—then shoot!

Vary the angles of your flash. You can obtain some interesting effects by bouncing the flash off light-colored surfaces when

167

working in close. Use the flash only for fill-in when employing black-and-white film.

Taking action pictures underwater is actually easier than filming above, for below the surface you rarely have to prompt the actors into motion. In fact, if there is a problem, it is just that—the photographer, too, tends to move!

Besides the 8 mm. or 16 mm. camera, you will of course need an underwater housing. There are as many of these available for cine-work as for still-photography, but one of the most sturdy cases is that made by Bolex for their 8 mm. and 16 mm. cameras—which are precision units in themselves—and equally adaptable to amateur and professional filming.

Use a fast wide-angle lens which allows you to move in closer to the subject. You can then shoot through less water and obtain a great angle of coverage. For the 8 mm., use a 5.5 mm. lens; a 10 mm. lens is ideal for use on the 16 mm. models. Remember that distances are magnified, so good depth of field is possible with these lenses of short focal length. Set the lens at about 4 feet and forget it.

As a general rule, just as you did in still-photography, open the lens at least one f/stop for each 10 feet you descend. The same light metre works for cine-work as for still-photography, so use it.

While color is certainly the choice for capturing the fantastic beauty of the underwater world, remember that black and white has its place in cine-pictures just as in still-photography. Lighting units are needed for depths below 30 feet, and can be synchronized to operate when the camera runs.

Learn to move through the water with a minimum of effort, without disturbing your surroundings. Moving smoothly through the water will enable you to "dolly" in on many subjects, giving a "zoom" effect to your completed footage. Pan slowly and hold scenes to at least 8 to 10 seconds duration, because your audience will not be as familiar with the watery environment as you are. Have your sequences tell a story; add comedy, human interest, excitement, and even drama, where possible. With a little practice in technique and a bit of editing, underwater cine-photography could well become your means of capturing the beauty of the sea, and preserving its magic for others.

Author Bill Slosky prepares for a day's filming underwater with his Nikonos camera. Flash bulbs are easily carried on a belt.

The greatest discoveries in the underwater in the future will be made by divers using scuba or aqualung equipment. These men belong to Le Club Méditerranée, Cadaques, Spain, one of the world's largest diving schools.

EXPANDING DEPTHS

As a snorkeler you have been enjoying many phases of underwater swimming—aided only by a mask, breathing-tube, and swim-fins. This, seemingly, could very well satisfy all of your diving ambitions, except one—duration. Even the greatest of free-divers have only $2\frac{1}{2}$ to 3 minutes bottom-time before they must surface, and hyperventilate again, for another dive. Very likely you are now eager and ready to experience aqualung diving.

The era of the aqualung diver was ushered in about 1946 when the self-contained breathing unit first reached the commercial market. The sport's fantastic growth has been international and can be attributed to its wide appeal to people of all ages and backgrounds.

The unique sensation of natural breathing while drifting through the underwater with all the freedom and mobility of a fish is a wonderful experience. Besides the sheer thrill of being in a totally foreign environment, tank-diving broadens practically every phase of free-diving by allowing you to go deeper

Beginners in scuba usually train first in a swimming pool, but fortunate novices start in safe, shallow bays or on beaches.

and stay longer. This added range in time and depth is a considerable benefit to exploration, photography, treasure diving, and specimen collecting.

Unlike snorkeling, which can be learned easily enough through reading and experience, tank-diving should not be attempted without the aid of a competent instructor who understands and can teach the laws pertaining to compressed-air breathing in the watery domain you are about to enter.

At Cadaques, Spain, on the Costa Brava near Port Bou, lies one of several diving villages of the French, Le Club Méditerranée. If you are fortunate enough to spend a two or three week "holiday" with Le Club, you will enjoy excellent diving in the deep blue Mediterranean waters. Much different from the southern Atlantic waters you have experienced throughout your snorkeling phases, the Mediterranean is less blue, the horizon more abrupt, the water seemingly weakened in distance and depth. Though truly grand, there is something hard in the profile of the rocks, the formation of grottoes and caverns.

Complete freedom of movement can be achieved easily while gliding along underwater with a compressed-air tank on your back.

There are fewer Sea Urchins, little vegetation, and none of the common Gorgonians. On the other hand, you will feel a certain sensation—almost like gooseflesh or pins and needles. There is a certain exhilaration, here, rarely felt in warm-water diving.

In addition to offering advanced diving for the expert, Le Club Méditerranée is best known for its training of novice divers. Knowing the basics of snorkeling, you can go through Le Club's five days of training with aqualungs and end your "holiday" stay with exploration dives to 131 feet! The French instructors are not only crack divers, but are considered by many to be the finest trained diving instructors in the world.

At each of Le Club's diving villages there is at least one doctor who specializes in diving physiology. Good health and a feeling of ease in the water are musts if you intend to spend prolonged periods of time underwater. Before you are allowed to begin your aqualung training, you will be given a thorough physical examination, with close attention to ears, nose, sinuses, throat,

Use of safety equipment is a must when using self-contained breathing apparatus. Here, a fully outfitted French diving instructor, wearing a Fenzy inflatable vest, climbs aboard Le Club Méditerranée training boat.

and lungs. Later you will be doing a great deal of grotto and cave diving, so the doctor will test your psychological reactions to darkness. A healthy diver is generally a safe diver!

Diving with Le Club Méditerranée is not simply a one-shot affair. Each year divers from all over the world spend several weeks at a different village. If you are planning to be in southern Europe, include a few weeks with Le Club—one of the best diving organizations available.

Off the southern coast of Spain, a very dangerous but lucrative profession from the sea thrives. Coral, not the reef-building varieties of tropical seas, but the beautiful semi-precious Red Coral is found in these Mediterranean waters. This coral was prized by the Greeks and Romans, and its value and beauty were even referred to in the Bible. The hard red stone is covered during the coral's life by a soft, bark-like crust. The inner core takes a high polish, and for thousands of years has been treasured for beads and rings.

For centuries, Red Coral was commercially dredged in the

Fingers and branches of Red Coral growing deep in a Mediterranean grotto lure adventurous coral divers seeking this highly prized treasure.

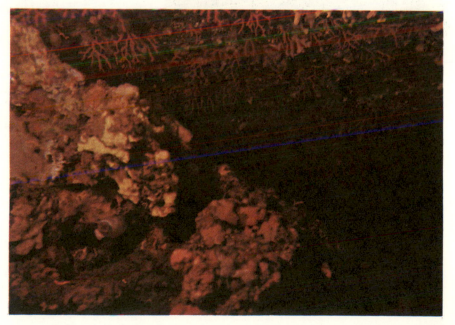

These men make their living diving for coral off the Mediterranean shores.

This professional diver watches his depth gauge continually as he works on extracting the Red Coral.

176

With torch strapped to wrist and gloved hand securing the mallet, this coral diver uses his free hand to dislodge the precious coral growth. Only with intense light are the reds evident.

Mediterranean with a type of wooden drag that smashed down the miniature trees and recovered a few branches. Coral that had taken hundreds of years to grow along the sea floor was destroyed for ever. The surviving coral grows below 120 feet in protected recesses and grottoes and can only be recovered by divers. At this depth the small branches resemble blue trees with pale white blossoms that retract and disappear when disturbed. A diver entering a coral cave must be aware of its appearance in the deceiving color filter of the sea. These divers are the Coral Fishermen of the Costa Brava.

Along the Mediterranean coast before 1960, anyone with an aqualung, a small boat, and a dream of fortune was diving for Red Coral. The world market was good. Divers knew that buyers from Italy, France, and Spain would take as much as they could supply, and supply they did.

The Spanish Government became concerned about the coral diving. Without some form of control, it would only be a

Since all coral divers work against time at critical depths, they must select the best grades to bring up. This diver is examining the quality of a small branch he has dislodged.

matter of time before the entire coast was fished out—which had happened in Italy. In 1961, the Spanish authorities set up strict regulations for those who dive for the precious red branches: now divers must be licensed and pay taxes on the coral they sell; and every three years the government closes one area and opens another for diving, thus allowing the coral to build up again.

In 1963, there were thirty coral fishermen on the Costa Brava; today there are fewer than ten!

Pedro and Eusebio live with their wives in the small fishing village of Port Illgat, made famous by the artist, Salvador Dali. At 7 o'clock each morning the two men take their diving

At a depth of 170 feet, the coral diver, with light attached to his waist, searches for new grottoes and more and better quality coral.

Decompressing on the way up, a coral diver hangs on the anchor-line of his craft. Carrying his loaded sack, he waits the time necessary to allow the nitrogen he has absorbed to dissipate through his blood.

At the end of the dive, the coral diver looks over the coral he has collected during his 15 minutes on the bottom.

tanks to the boat of a friend; in less than an hour Pedro and Eusebio will be at depths of 180 to 280 feet, searching for first-class Red Coral. Size, color, and thickness of the branches determine the class of the corals. Pedro once brought up a single piece that sold for $130 (£46), but that came from 287 feet—a depth where rapture turns one's imagination to fantasies. Who knows what would have happened had Eusebio not insisted he return to the anchor-line for the all-important decompression. Danger for the coral divers means *time*. It will sneak up on them, trick them, and pass them by. After spending only thirty minutes at 200 feet, the divers must immediately ascend to various markers on their boat's anchor-line for required decompression stops totalling more than an hour! But it must be worth the danger—Pedro and Eusebio are still among The Coral Fishermen of the Costa Brava.

For some time, the concept of establishing underwater parks as natural reserves has intrigued underwater sportsmen, naturalists, and photographers. Game and commercial fishes would be free to replenish their numbers in a protected element, and, later on, they would stock non-protected surrounding areas. This would guarantee constant supplies to sportsmen upon whom large sporting industries and tourism are dependent, and a natural out-of-doors laboratory would be provided for scientists, educators, and all those who enjoy the wonders of nature.

For the general public, interest in significant coral gardens marine life, and the aesthetic values of an undersea wilderness unspoiled by trapfishing, sportfishing, spearfishing, or even souvenir treasure hunters (who often take small pieces of coral or sea fans), has brought about the establishment of several underwater sanctuaries. A great many other marine areas are under consideration, and though most of the present marine reserves are co-operatively sanctioned by U.S. Federal and State governments, a few Caribbean areas have been unofficially protected for some time.

Buck Island Reef National Monument was established in 1961, but the island has been under the control of the Virgin Islands Government since 1936. The sun-swept island, located

The popularity of group diving is being further encouraged by the establishment of underwater parks and trails. These divers are about to start on a day's safari by seaplane.

Equipment in hand, the snorkeler above hops from the seaplane into the water where he will don his gear. The young lady below will drop to a raft, which already is equipped with a lunch package.

five miles west of St. Croix, is significantly different from adjacent islands in this part of the West Indies. Surrounding the eastern half of Buck Island is a magnificent barrier reef, a continuous coral barrier that lies offshore, separated by an emerald clear lagoon.

With the increasing popularity of skin diving, more and more snorkelers and scuba divers are discovering the marine gardens through self-guiding underwater nature trails with submerged plaques providing information about the marine life to be seen in the underwater fairyland.

The first marker on the trail indicates the direction to follow.

As you glide over the protected reef, you will find yourself surrounded by fish you know, but also many others new to you. The first grouper is always one to remember—upright on its tail, in front of the sandy little ground-floor grotto, its enormous gills so out of proportion to the stocky body. The eyes, lurking deep in the bony orbits seem very intent, and you sense the backward spring for which it is ready at the first hint that you might dive on it. Then suddenly it catapults backwards—only a tiny cloud of sand settling back again in front of the lair.

Markers line the trail, providing snorkelers with information about the marine life to be seen along the underwater way.

A snorkeling promenade through an underwater park is suggestive of a visit to a village square: everywhere there is color and motion. You will see gaudy green and blue Parrot-fishes grazing on algae, and Wrasses with the teeth of parrots, set in oval plates, and large scales of semi-tropical coloring: astonishing shades of red, ochre, and pearl grey, spotted with all possible colors, some of them bi-colored. Hold out your hand. If the gesture is as slow as a fish's swimming, the fish may halt so close that you can almost touch it.

Large schools of Grunts and Snappers are assembled in protected areas, resting from the night's foraging. Little Damsel-fish guard their chosen plots of coral, and Neon Gobies briskly remove the skin parasites of passing reef inhabitants. Lonely Angelfishes—Black, Queen, and French, in many shades, swim by as the colorful Wrasses scuddle about constantly near the reef. Brilliant Demoiselles seem suspended over masses of Brain and Finger Coral, and a peculiar Trumpetfish may be seen standing on his head among the soft coral Sea Whips.

Bright red Squirrel Fishes dart in and out among openings in the coral.

Then come the Mackerel, swimming the length of the reef. Another day, another place, you might hunt them by diving down to the bottom, then remaining poised, horizontal for a moment to get a good aim at their own level. But, here, on this reserve you only marvel at their bodies which are large and metallic—more like missiles than fish. A shoal of small semi-transparent fish, a couple of inches long, are seemingly glued one to another as if actuated by one single force. These Silversides are often followed by many free-swimming fishes. Parties of young Angelfishes flutter over the rocks. Their brilliant, rounded bodies have transverse bands which separate one shade of blue or black from another.

Besides the swimming creatures, there is a rich, vast undersea acreage of coral formations, a fabulous platform of fingers, platters, fans, and clumps. Branching Elkhorn Coral, willowy Sea Fans and Sea Feathers, quaint sponges, and armored crustaceans. And the Sea Urchins! It is, in fact, the little things here that one needs to beware of. For instance, it is interesting to see how black Sea Urchins defend themselves. They seemingly send out a shower of shafts, as if blown by invisible breath from a pea-shooter.

Familiarity with these forms of marine life makes your trip through the underwater park much more exciting, and the fascinating cycle of animal life that exists in this underwater sanctuary will amaze and delight you.

Today, in oceans around the world, experiments and technological advances are taking place that give us greater insight into oceanography. Within the next few years, world-wide spending on underwater research is expected to equal or even exceed the current effort going into missiles and space research, and it is felt that the returns may be many times greater and come sooner than even the most optimistic forecasts of dividends from space.

In Cousteau-inspired underwater villages, aquanauts are spending weeks at a time living among the fishes in undersea dwellings. Though these experiments are not directly related to underwater swimming as we know it, the outcome of the projects will ultimately influence the types of underwater equipment made available to sport divers.

A few years back, much of the gear now in use for underwater recreation was used exclusively by the military. Communication equipment is now available whereby audible speech is made possible between divers, as well as between surface and diver.

Fantastic as it may seem, artificial gills have been designed which enable man to breathe underwater like a fish! The diver is able to obtain the necessary oxygen from water and to dispose of his exhaled carbon dioxide in the same medium. A permeable microporous membrane allows oxygen to be drawn in and carbon dioxide to be discharged, but prevents liquids (water) from entering. The diver is able to breathe because the water pressure on the gill bag containing the recirculated air is equalized by the water pressure on his rib cage.

Not too many years ago some noted authorities in the field of underwater research speculated that one day surgeons would equip human beings with gills, thereby changing them into "men-fishes." No one can deny that this looms as possibly the next step in our evolution back to the sea.

Though expensive, undoubtedly the best method devised for natural vision underwater has been the full contact lens. Unlike the small corneal or micro lenses which are easily lost when swimming, the larger optic lenses are held firmly by the lids, even with the eyes open underwater.

The nearsighted or farsighted diver who needs a prescription can have this incorporated into his contact lenses. Obtaining complete peripheral vision is perhaps the major advantage of the new lenses. The most commonly voiced criticism of swim-masks is their restriction of wide-angle viewing. With the new contact lens being manufactured from unshatterable plastic that is on par, optically, with good glass, a diver can focus as well through them above water as below.

For the underwater photographer, viewing through contact lenses enables him to focus properly through the camera's view-finder without the usual blocking of the face-mask.

What does the diving future hold for you? You have seen that man can make the whole marine world his, so the decision is yours to make.

Soon many people may be using contact lenses in preference to a face-mask. This French diver looks "bug-eyed" as he descends with contact lenses in place.

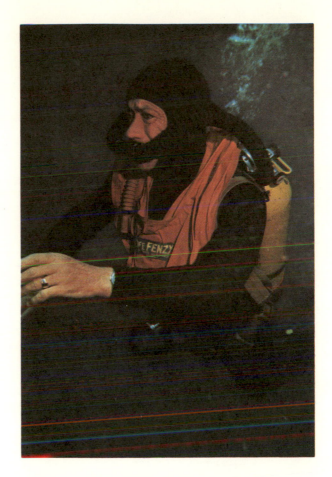

PHOTOGRAPHIC DATA FOR ALL PHOTOGRAPHS IN THIS BOOK
EXPOSED UNDERWATER

Using Nikonos Camera—lens 35 mm., Ektachrome X film, and flash lighting, except where noted as follows:

AL — Available lighting   P — Plus X film
K — Kodachrome II film   AG — Agfachrome film

PAGE	EXPOSURE	DEPTH	PAGE	EXPOSURE	DEPTH
8	1/125 f/5.6	70'	56	1/125 f/4	65'
9	1/125 f/4	15'		1/125 f/4	10'
10	1/125 f/5	70'	58	1/125 f/11	15'
12	1/125 f/5.6	40'	59	1/125 f/4	140'
13	1/125 f/5	65'		1/125 f/5.6	15'
15	1/250 f/3	10'	60	1/125 f/5.6	10'
16	1/125 f/4	8'	61	1/125 f/8	8'
20	1/250 f/5.6	4'		1/125 f/5.6	12'
	1/250 f/5.6	4'	62	1/125 f/8 AL	7'
21	1/250 f/8	4'	63	1/125 f/5.6	10'
22	1/250 f/8	5'		1/125 f/5.6	12'
23	1/125 f/4	20'	64	1/125 f/4	15'
27	1/125 f/5.6	25'	65	1/125 f/5.6	70'
28	1/125 f/5.6	40'	66	1/125 f/4	160'
29	1/125 f/4	70'	67	1/125 f/4	20'
30	1/125 f/5.6	35'		1/125 f/8	25'
31	1/125 f/4	55'	69	1/125 f/5.6	40'
32	1/125 f/8	4'		1/125 f/11	30'
34	1/125 f/2.5	40'	70	1/125 f/8	10'
35	1/125 f/8 K, AL	4'	71	1/125 f/4	70'
37	1/125 f/4	80'		1/125 f/5.6	15'
40	1/125 f/8	3'	72	1/125 f/5.6	15'
	1/125 f/8	25'		1/125 f/5.6 K, AL	12'
42	1/125 f/8	30'	73	1/125 f/5.6	20'
43	1/125 f/8	15'	75	1/125 f/5.6	8'
44	1/125 f/5.6	30'		1/125 f/8	30'
	1/125 f/5.6	35'	76	1/125 f/8	25'
45	1/125 f/5.6	15'	77	1/125 f/4	15'
46	1/125 f/8	25'		1/125 f/8	15'
47	1/125 f/8	25'	78	1/125 f/5.6	20'
48	1/250 f/4	65'		1/125 f/8	10'
49	1/125 f/5.6	15'	79	1/125 f/8	35'
	1/125 f/4	35'	80	1/250 f/2.5	70'
50	1/250 f/2.5 AG	50'	81	1/125 f/2.5	30'
	1/125 f/5.6	25'		1/125 f/5.6	50'
51	1/125 f/4	70'	82	1/125 f/5.6	35'
53	1/125 f/4	30'		1/125 f/5.6	135'
	1/125 f/8	15'	84	1/125 f/5.6	12'
54	1/125 f/8	20'	85	1/125 f/8	15'
55	1/125 f/4	15'		1/125 f/5.6	25'

PAGE	EXPOSURE	DEPTH	PAGE	EXPOSURE	DEPTH
86	1/125 f/2.5	30′	134	1/125 f/5.6	45′
	1/125 f/4	45′	135	1/125 f/4	17′
87	1/125 f/5.6	25′	136	1/125 f/8	15′
88	1/125 f/5.6	65′		1/125 f/8	10′
89	1/125 f/4	10′	138	1/250 f/3.5	75′
90	1/125 f/11 AL	12′	140	1/125 f/2.5	80′
91	1/125 f/4	8′	141	1/250 f/3.5	45′
	1/125 f/8	4′	142	1/125 f/4	80′
92	1/125 f/5.6	15′		1/125 f/4	40′
	1/125 f/5.6	35′	143	1/125 f/5.6	70′
94	1/125 f/8	8′	145	1/125 f/2.5	80′
95	1/125 f/5.6	15′	146	1/125 f/4	30′
96	1/125 f/8	9′	147	1/125 f/8	75′
	1/125 f/8	10′		1/125 f/4	80′
98	1/125 f/4	15′	148	1/125 f/5.6	15′
100	1/125 f/5.6	15′	149	1/125 f/5.6	15′
101	1/125 f/5.6	12′		1/125 f/8	8′
103	1/125 f/5.6	7′	153	1/125 f/4	8′
104	1/125 f/5.6	8′	154	1/250 f/4	65′
106	1/125 f/4	15′	156	1/125 f/4	60′
107	1/125 f/5.6	15′	157	1/125 f/5.6	75′
108	1/125 f/11 AL	10′	158	1/125 f/3 AL	20′
109	1/125 f/5.6	9′	159	1/125 f/3.5	50′
110	1/250 f/4	7′	160	1/125 f/4	15′
111	1/125 f/8	10′	161	1/125 f/5.6	60′
113	1/125 f/4	15′	162	1/125 f/5.6	35′
114	1/125 f/8	15′	163	1/125 f/5.6	30′
116	1/125 f/5.6	12′	165	1/125 f/4	160′
117	1/125 f/5.6	9′	166	1/250 f/5.6	25′
120	1/125 f/5.6	40′		1/250 f/5.6	25′
122	1/125 f/5.6	10′	167	1/250 f/5.6	25′
123	1/125 f/8	30′	173	1/125 f/4	45′
124	1/125 f/8	15′	175	1/125 f/2.5	185′
125	1/125 f/4	15′	176	1/125 f/8 P	170′
126	1/125 f/4	25′	177	1/125 f/3	190′
127	1/125 f/8	20′	178	1/125 f/3	165′
128	1/125 f/5.6	18′	179	1/125 f/8 P	130′
129	1/125 f/8	35′		1/125 f/8 P, AL	15′
130	1/125 f/8	20′	183	1/125 f/5.6	10′
131	1/125 f/5.6	15′	184	1/125 f/5.6	15′
132	1/125 f/4	55′	187	1/125 f/5.6	25′
133	1/125 f/5.6	60′			
	1/125 f/8	45′			

UNDERWATER
COLOR CORRECTION FILTER CHART
(RED)

Absorbs blue and green

Distance to Subject	Filter	Exposure Increase in Stops
1 ft.	CC–05R	1/3
2–3 ft.	CC–10R	1/3
4–6 ft.	CC–20R	1/3
7–8 ft.	CC–30R	2/3
9–11 ft.	CC–40R	2/3
12–13 ft.	CC–50R	1

UNDERWATER
COLOR CORRECTION FILTER CHART
(MAGENTA)

Absorbs green

Distance to Subject	Filter	Exposure Increase in Stops
1 ft.	CC–05M	1/3
2–3 ft.	CC–10M	1/3
4–6 ft.	CC–20M	1/3
7–8 ft.	CC–30M	2/3
9–11 ft.	CC–40M	2/3
12–13 ft.	CC–50M	2/3

NIKONOS
COLOR FILM FLASH EXPOSURE CHART (ASA 64)
(FOCAL PLANE SHUTTER)

Distance to Subject	# 6 or 26 Clear bulbs Guide #80
4 ft.	1/125 f/11
6 ft.	1/125 f/6.3
8 ft.	1/125 f/5.6
10 ft.	1/125 f/8

Index